SAVING ANNE THE ELEPHANT

CLAIRE ELLICOTT

SAVING ANNE THE ELEPHANT

THE TRUE STORY OF THE LAST BRITISH CIRCUS ELEPHANT

JOHN BLAKE

Published by John Blake Publishing Ltd,
3 Bramber Court, 2 Bramber Road,
London W14 9PB, England

www.johnblakebooks.com

www.facebook.com/johnblakebooks
twitter.com/jblakebooks

This edition published in 2016

ISBN: 978 1 78418 977 8

British Library Cataloguing-in-Publication Data:

A catalogue record for this book is available from the British Library.

Design by www.envydesign.co.uk

Printed in Great Britain by CPI Group (UK) Ltd

1 3 5 7 9 10 8 6 4 2

Papers used by John Blake Publishing are natural, recyclable products made from wood grown in sustainable forests. The manufacturing processes conform to the environmental regulations of the country of origin.

CONTENTS

ACKNOWLEDGEMENTS

Thank you to my mother, my father and my sister for their love and support.

Many thanks to ADI, Longleat, the Robertses and my other interviewees for enduring my endless questions and queries. And thanks to the *Daily Mail* for encouraging me to write this book.

PROLOGUE

It was a crisp night in January. Outside, the stars were twinkling and the residents of the sleepy village of Polebrook in rural Northamptonshire were settling down for the night. All except for one. In a large and stuffy metal hangar, surrounded by stables crammed with camels, horses and miniature ponies, Anne, Britain's last circus elephant, was chained to the spot by her front and hind leg. Defenceless and numb, she awaited yet another attack by the cruel groom who had terrorised her for months. Her existence was pitiful and squalid and had changed little in the fifty years she had spent at Bobby Roberts Super Circus. Locked away in the dim and crowded barn in the circus winter quarters, the only break from the monotony was the regular abuse she endured. But no one knew what her life was like or what she suffered until an investigator from an animal rights campaign group sneaked a camera into her barn. He planted the pinhole device in a hole in the back wall of the shed and let it run for three weeks. Though the group were well used to seeing horrific animal abuse images, the footage shocked even them. Anne's groom, a Romanian man named Nicolae Nitu, twenty-five, who had been hired to muck out the stables, was subjecting her to the most appalling assaults.

Day after day, he was filmed entering her barn and attacking her, stabbing her in the face with a pitchfork, beating her around the head with metal staves and kicking her severely arthritic leg, which she still drags behind her. The violence was casual, arbitrary and entirely unprovoked. She was hit no fewer than forty-eight times. The mighty creature was shown wincing in pain and cowering from her attacker every time he entered the barn. At one point, she seemed to wet herself in fear. At another, she tried to escape but the chains she endured all day, every day, kept her rooted to the spot. And though elephants have thick skin, there can be no doubt that she suffered. Her arthritic leg nearly gave way several times under the force.

And she wasn't the only animal he attacked. Nitu, who couldn't speak English and was simply known as 'Jimmy' at the circus because no one could say his name, was shown kicking and beating ponies and spitting in camels' faces. But most of his rage was reserved for Anne. In one clip, he is shown raking the hay near her while she stands next to him, motionless. Suddenly, he picks up the pitchfork and wallops her on her arthritic leg. It is an act of wanton cruelty that no normal human being could bear to watch without stepping in. But no one was there to step in and no one came to save her. Her owner, Bobby, entered the barn just four times during the three weeks of filming. His wife Moira didn't go once. When Bobby did go in, he was wearing a suit. The film shows him looking at her, his hands on his hips, as she stares back at him. Then he walks off camera to her side and Anne is shown forlornly, tentatively, reaching out her trunk to him. But he kicks it away and she recoils.

The footage, which is now world-famous, is heart-breaking. But what is most heartbreaking of all is the everyday life she endured. Shackled to the floor by chains in a dank barn with a meagre scattering of hay for most of the year and wheeled out to perform tricks in front of crowds for the rest, she knew little else during her fifty years with the circus. Unable to move more than one pace in any direction, she developed a habit of swaying from side-to-side and lifting her trunk and leg in what animal behaviourists call stereotypic behaviour.

Vets think the crippling arthritis that hampers her every movement and causes her to drag her back leg is almost certainly a result of her circus performances.

Forced to rear on her hind legs and balance on a tub for matinee and then evening shows, she has permanent damage to her frame, they say.

For the short breaks in between her performances, she was chained to a wooden pallet on the ground outside in a tiny area. With no prospect of relief from the doleful life of boredom and humiliation, the days will no doubt have blended into one. And while she had clear physical ailments as a result, she was also suffering psychologically. When she arrived at Longleat, vets said she was suffering the animal equivalent of post-traumatic stress. Her osteopath said her eyes had lost their sparkle.

Though many have seen the edited online footage, which focuses only on the violence meted out to her, few have seen the endless hours during which Anne was chained to the floor, which was her true day-to-day existence. Even now, when she is free from the circus and living in retirement in a place that caters to her every need, she still exhibits the same compulsive, stereotypic behaviour. It is a powerful reminder of how, just like humans, animals can suffer psychological damage.

That damage would have started young. Born in Sri Lanka, she was taken from her mother at the age of about four. There is disagreement over whether she was wild or captive-born, but had she been the former, she would have had to be 'broken' – an horrific process that involves putting an elephant in a crush (a small pen bordered with logs) and denying it food until its spirit is broken and it becomes entirely subservient to its human controllers.

She was then bought by Bobby Roberts' father and shipped over to England. She was later inherited by his son and spent fifty years with the family circus performing pirouettes, standing on tubs and galloping round the ring with dancers on her back. In her many years at the circus, she was fed by Her Majesty The Queen, went up the Eiffel Tower and featured on a special edition of the BBC's *Songs of Praise*. A regular on television, she has also starred in films, adverts and music videos. But as public opinion began to turn against wild animals in circuses, the number of performing elephants in the UK decreased until it was just Anne. Animal rights groups bided their time until Animal Defenders International (ADI) uncovered the footage that changed everything.

Desperate to free her, the pressure group handed the footage to the *Daily Mail*, who, day after day, ran a high profile and unrelenting campaign for her rescue. I, a reporter for the newspaper, broke the story with my colleague Chris Greenwood and visited Anne, the circus and the winter quarters, reporting on the rapidly developing story.

Meanwhile, back at the circus, the groom had already fled to his native Romania. He has never been brought to justice because he cannot be extradited. Animal cruelty is judged to be such a minor offence that there is no warrant for his arrest.

His departure meant much of the anger was directed at the Robertses, who were still travelling with their circus. Fury erupted across the country and the circus was picketed everywhere it went. Meanwhile, Anne was still at the winter quarters and still chained to the ground. Behind the scenes, the newspaper, animal rights organisations and safari parks were all frantically trying to find a way to save her from her miserable condition. Over the following days, public pressure on her owners grew from a din to a roar and Bobby was persuaded to let her go. A plan was agreed to send her to Longleat Safari Park & Adventure Park in Wiltshire, where she could at last retire and enjoy her life.

Despite warnings that her pain was so great and her condition so bad that she might have to be put down, Anne was rescued. Accorded the same status as a Category A prisoner, she was transported to her new home under police guard. She now lives in a luxury £1.2 million elephant house partly funded by charitable donations from *Daily Mail* readers. Her story captured the nation's hearts and she became a famous figure and was visited by actor Russell Crowe and naturalist Sir David Attenborough in her new home.

Meanwhile, the Robertses denied all the allegations of cruelty and claimed that Anne was 'one of the family' and would 'pine away and die' were she to be separated from Bobby. Bobby said that he was world-renowned for his animal husbandry and was called the 'elephant man' because of his talents. But both were later charged with animal cruelty and appeared in court in 2012. Bobby was convicted of causing unnecessary suffering to Anne by chaining her to the floor at all times, failing to prevent her groom from beating her and failing to ensure her needs were met but was controversially let off with a suspended sentence. He wasn't banned from keeping animals nor was he fined.

It is undeniable that Anne suffered at the hands of her groom, but she never once complained during her terrible suffering. The dull thwack of the metal on her flanks as her groom beat her was almost the only sound on the video. Perhaps she didn't want to react in case it provoked him to further violence. Or maybe she'd simply learned that there was no point – no one would help her anyway. Either way, it adds poignancy to her story that she suffered in silence, retaining her dignity in the face of a series of brutal and arbitrary assaults.

Mother Nature has created few things more awe-inspiring and majestic than the elephant. Perhaps that's why her incredible story won over the nation. It is now almost universally agreed upon that elephants, our biggest land mammal, shouldn't perform in circuses and the British Government has promised to make it illegal in the future. Anne's awful suffering was one of the catalysts for the ban and her legacy, told in this book, should be to ensure wild animals never have to perform in circuses ever again. The following is the true story of her horrific suffering during her time at the circus and her eventual liberation and the start of her new life.

CHAPTER 1

FALLOUT FROM THE STORY, MY FIRST MEETING WITH ANNE AND CIRCUS PROTESTS

Anne was once a big star. People flocked from all over the country to see her and her fellow elephants perform in the greatest show on earth. Crowds lined the streets to greet her as she paraded from the train station to the showground to announce the arrival of the circus in town. Adorned in exotic headgear, she pirouetted and balanced on a tub to the roar of the crowd in the Big Top. Her photo was pasted on billboards and children queued to have their picture taken with her. During an extraordinary life, she met royalty, paraded through the main streets of Europe and performed for heads of state. She lived through the golden age of the Great British Circus when it dominated the television schedules and elephants jostled with brightly-painted clowns and daring trapeze artists for the spotlight. It was a time when tigers jumped through flaming hoops and sea lions clapped for the crowds.

That starry life seemed a very distant memory when I first met the elderly Anne in the metal hangar she called home at her winter quarters in Polebrook, Northamptonshire. Bobby had invited me down the day after the terrible crimes against her were exposed. There was a scattering of hay across the floor and, in one corner, ankles in chains, was Anne. Hearing our approach, she made her way towards us, dragging her severely arthritic leg. Although slow and deliberate, she quickly gathered pace and her eyes twinkled.

Bobby handed me some Warburtons bread to feed her. It was extraordinary to stand next to such an exotic and otherworldly creature in what looked like an agricultural yard in the Northamptonshire countryside. Impatient with me, her trunk darted from my hand to the packet, pinching as much bread as possible.

Standing below her, I was struck by her size and how human her reactions seemed to be. More of a cheeky toddler than an ageing elephant, she is thought, if calculations are correct, to be the oldest elephant in Europe. She survived five decades in the circus performing tricks and, in her later years, was rolled out to pose for photos with children. The year her dreadful suffering was exposed was the first time she had stayed behind at the winter quarters and not gone on tour with the circus. Lonely and constantly chained to the floor, and with just her cruel groom for company, she must have suffered even more.

Unbeknownst to her owners, animal rights group ADI (Animal Defenders International) had planted a secret camera in her barn. They passed the shocking footage to the newspaper. The previous night, I had been sent to Knutsford, Cheshire to find the Bobby Roberts Super Circus on the first night of its tour to give Moira and Bobby their right to respond to our story. When I arrived, the circus was just beginning the evening performance. I was quickly directed to Moira, who was taking money at the gates, and she agreed to speak to me. We went to one of the trailers and Bobby joined us afterwards. I played them both the footage that had been taken by ADI.

During an emotional, and at times angry, interview the Robertses talked to me about their lives with Anne and what she meant to them. Bobby, a short and stout man with heavy greyish-ginger sideburns and thick eyebrows, was indignant and hostile. Wearing his circus outfit – a suit with a white jacket, a black bow tie and a white, spangly waistcoat – he paced and shouted, throwing his hands up in disbelief at what had happened. He had to leave halfway through the interview to continue as ringmaster in the Big Top – the show had to go on. His wife Moira, small and with thick-rimmed glasses, was defiant and proud, not giving any ground. The couple swore that they had never mistreated Anne.

During our interview, I asked Bobby about one scene in the footage in which someone kicks her trunk. The person is off camera and cannot be seen properly. ADI had made an accusation that Bobby had kicked her, to which he responded: 'It's disgusting! I have never kicked Anne. They can accuse me as much as they like. She's part of the family. I'm disgusted.' He added of Anne's groom, Nicolae Nitu: 'He's going. I can't believe this has happened under my nose. His duty was to look after Anne. We trusted him and we'd check on her every hour or so. I can't be there twenty-four hours a day. The boy is going to be fired tonight.' He even accused ADI of planting the groom who abused her, in order to get Anne out of the circus: 'The last time I saw this they [the groom] were paid to do this.' Moira said that the pitchfork used by the groom was plastic and the metal thwacking sounds on the video were dubbed over later. Moira told me: 'The man will be sacked. Soon as we get back he will sacked on the spot.'

Moira said that they left Anne behind that year because it was bad weather and they left Nitu to care for her. They had been planning to fetch her when the weather improved and her arthritis was bothering her less, she says.

By the time I had arrived at the vast circus grounds the next morning, Nitu was long gone, tipped off somehow despite the story only breaking in our newspaper that morning and him not being able to speak English.

The farm is in the genteel village of Polebrook, which is home to an historic listed hall which was used as a headquarters by the RAF during the Second World War. The Hollywood actor Clark Gable flew missions from the base in 1943. The circus grounds are almost opposite the hall. I arrived not knowing what to expect. The winter quarters looked more like a salvage yard than a circus and a few brightly-coloured lorries were the only clues to its main use. The atmosphere felt hostile and everyone was on edge. Bobby took me to see Anne. Wearing a brown and grey striped cardigan and a black baseball cap with flaps at the side to keep his ears warm, he took me to her enclosure, telling me that she was coming up to sixty. Calling her his 'old lady', he told of the last time he saw her before footage of the abuse was released. 'The vet came past before we left,' he said. 'I know every bit of her and she's fine. There are no marks.'

He told me how zoos would come to him for advice on not just elephants but pigs, horses, camels and tigers, and that he had once trained four tigers himself. When I asked him about the training, he answered: 'It takes a long time. All people say is it's cruel to do this. How many people have a dog that will fetch? Even children have to be trained.' He also said that to protect himself and others, he had to restrain Anne so she would often be chained and kept in her enclosure surrounded by an electric fence. 'Sometimes we had her on a chain. I had her on one. There is a chain running between all the boards,' he said.

During the same interview, Bobby also argued passionately that circuses weren't cruel to animals and that there was nothing wrong with the way animals were treated in them. 'I don't think there's anything cruel [in the circus]. We have a strict code for animal welfare.' He said that animal welfare officers 'always come and check. They say to me some of these animals are kept in better conditions than what they are in stables.' When asked if he would ever consider handing Anne over to an animal sanctuary, he said: 'If the circumstances were right, I would part from her. But she would pine like I would.'

'It will break his heart to part with her,' said Moira. 'She'd pine away and die.' But they refused to allow her to go abroad: 'We won't let her go to the US because she won't last the journey. If there's a sanctuary over in the US, the journey would kill her. We have approached them [the sanctuary]. We have talked about it.'

Bobby added: 'They're not going to take an old elephant.' Moira agreed: 'She's an old, old lady now. The vet says she is worn out. We don't think she could stand the journey. We have spoken about this. Anne's worked hard for us all her life and we feel like we have to work hard to keep her comfortable.'

While I was at Polebrook speaking to Bobby, the country was waking up to the news of Anne's sad life.

Her picture was on the front page of the *Daily Mail* with the words: 'Exclusive: Torture of Britain's Last Circus Elephant'. Inside, the headline was: 'Anne's Agony: Battered, kicked and stabbed, the desperate plight of Britain's last circus elephant.' ADI were quoted on the incredible feat that they had pulled off. Jan told us: 'Poor Anne has been with the circus for over fifty years since she was a baby, having been caught in the wild and torn from her family. Elephants are social and extremely intelligent so this has been a living hell for her. At last we have managed to expose the circus operation for the cruel farce that it is. Anne's tragic story symbolises the plight of circus animals and is a shocking indictment of the circus.' Outraged at her treatment, scores of protesters then descended on the circus, demanding Anne be set free.

In the following days, the circus was picketed everywhere it went. Moira said the couple were under siege. She told me she had received death and kidnap threats and had contacted the police, who had taken a statement from her. She also told me that she'd given the details of the groom to the police, but they could not find him. She said at the time: 'I have emails where our children's lives have been threatened with kidnap. Bobby has been threatened with being shot. I'm trying to be strong, it's not easy. The strain on us has been unimaginable. We just don't know if our nerves can take any more.'

In an attempt to stem the vitriol, the family posted a statement on their website saying that they 'shared the public's outrage'. It read: 'Anne has been with us for fifty-five years, not just as a performing animal but as a family pet. She has been trained through kindness and reward to willingly obey gentle, spoken commands. She is now an elderly lady.' Next, it addressed Bobby's 'unblemished career' and added: 'He is deeply saddened that Anne, for whom he has deep affection, and who clearly loves Bobby, should have in any way suffered.' But the protests, led by the Captive Animals Protection Society (CAPS), continued and followed the circus on its tour.

As a result of the backlash, the Robertses had to erect metal security barriers around the Big Top. Moira said at the time that the girl manning the box office had received death threats. Bookings had also fallen 99 per cent, she added. They were forced to sell heavily-discounted tickets for the two-hour show to those brave enough to make it past the picket lines. Bobby told the *Blackpool Gazette* when they arrived there: 'We've had death threats, been frightened to let our grandchildren out of our sight.' He said that at one point a man had phoned to ask how close his seat was to the ring because he had brought a gun to shoot Bobby.

'We're not some big corporate with lots of money,' argued Moira, 'we're a traditional family circus. We haven't had a holiday in forty-five years, we won't leave our animals for longer than twenty-four hours, we're up against rising costs and red tape, the worst economy we've known, and other circuses going for the same business.' Days later, she told the *Observer*: 'We've always been proud of our name, but we feel it has been blackened. As a family we feel finished.'

The RSPCA was deluged by calls from members of the public demanding it check on Anne's health and sent Tim Bouts, at the time the head vet at Whipsnade Zoo. Questions were immediately asked about whether the Robertses had been giving Anne proper medication to cope with her arthritis, with which she was diagnosed in 2003. David Field, zoological director of the Zoological Society of London (ZSL), which includes Whipsnade, warned that the examination raised 'major questions' about the standard of care Anne had received for arthritis. He said: 'The vet who examined her found that she was a very sick animal with severe arthritis. It is not something that sets in quickly. She will have suffered with this for a long time and we are concerned that she may not have had the correct treatment. Major questions need to be asked about the care she's received over a prolonged period of time.'

Northamptonshire Constabulary working alongside the RSPCA also began an inquiry into what happened in the video with a view to prosecution.

Meanwhile, there was increasing political pressure on the British government to do something about Anne's plight and prevent it from happening again by banning the use of wild animals in circuses. Just days after the footage was released in March 2011, actor Brian Blessed, an ADI supporter, marched on Downing Street to demand that Prime Minister David Cameron bring in the ban. He said: 'The abuse suffered by this elephant by those that claim to care for her is outrageous. I am here today to make my feelings known to politicians and whoever else will listen to bring this appalling suffering to an end. It really is time for the government to do the right thing for these circus animals and finally implement a ban. We have been sitting on the fence for far too long, the suffering is terrible as clearly evidenced in this disgraceful video. It is unbelievable that wild animal circuses still exist in the UK and now is the time for the government to legislate and put a stop, once and for all, to the draconian and humiliating spectacle of wild animals in circuses.'

At the time of the march, more than 100,000 people had watched the ADI footage of Anne being battered, kicked and stabbed on YouTube. The organisation's public relations man Phil Buckley said at the time: 'We have had a lot of people phoning us in tears after seeing this.'

When the circus reached Knutsford, Cheshire, the public protests had intensified, and as the workers set up for the day, throngs of protesters numbering around 100 arrived outside the ground. A memorable picture from the time was of Gabriel Ryan, a four-year-old, who was accompanied by his mother. His face painted like a sad clown, he held a sign saying: 'Animals take the smiles out of the circus.' His mother, Sally Anne Ryan, said they had travelled from Wales to protest, saying: 'Having animals in a circus is an economic decision and we think it is cruel and unnecessary. The pictures of the poor elephant illustrated how they are kept and the treatment meted out to them.'

On that day, Wednesday, 31 March 2011, Moira told me that she blamed herself, as she had hired Nitu: 'I hired the man. I'm responsible. I thought I was a good judge of character. I'm not. I have completely lost all my faith in human beings. I hired him and I should not have done so.' She also said Bobby had been 'vilified' since the footage emerged and had received death threats.

Meanwhile, behind the scenes negotiations had resulted in an agreement for Anne to be moved to Longleat. Moira said of the move: 'As we had hoped, Anne will go to a retirement home where she will be looked after. We can have access as often as we like and she is going with our blessing. She is not being taken away from us. She is going where we want her to go and this is something we have wanted for the last two years.'

The couple invited villagers from Polebrook to say goodbye to Anne. Small groups went to the circus quarters carrying baskets of fruit as a farewell gesture. A family friend of the couple, who did not wish to be named, said: 'It's a sad day for many of us. There have been elephants in the village for sixty years.' But for the Robertses the pressures weren't over. ADI announced that they would be pursuing a private prosecution against the couple with the hope that the Crown Prosecution Service would take over, which is what eventually happened.

Finally, after decades of trying, the public pressure on the Robertses had worked and Anne was to be set free. But the next stage was ensuring that she was healthy enough to be moved. Her back leg was in a terrible state and she was old and had suffered for a long time. And the issue of where she might go was being hotly debated. There was a suggestion that she could go to ZSL Whipsnade Zoo, which had an existing herd of elephants she could be introduced to. Sanctuaries in the US offered her a home too. Meanwhile, MPs tabled a motion in Parliament calling on the government to deliver Anne from the squalor and cramped conditions in which she lived. But there were also murmurs about her going to Longleat Safari Park & Adventure Park as a temporary measure so she could have her health checked and tests done in quarantine before any decisions were made about her future.

Following the examination carried out by his vet Tim Bouts, David Field said: 'Fundamentally, Anne can be rehomed. The biggest and most important thing for her is she needs specialist veterinary care. Her physical state may not be very strong and a quick assessment of her arthritis may show that she is even so bad, she needs to be put down.' But he also said that everyone was hopeful that she would be moved from the circus within days. Things were suddenly looking up.

CHAPTER TWO

STORY OF ADI SNEAKING IN TO FILM HER AND RELEASE OF THE FOOTAGE TO THE PAPER

Animal Defenders International (ADI) is the campaign group that began the quest to free Anne. Having previously exposed animal suppliers Mary Chipperfield Promotions Ltd – a name which has since become synonymous with animal cruelty – they had been trying for more than fifteen years to rescue the elephant. Jan Creamer and her husband Tim Phillips are the colourful couple who run the small but ambitious group that travels the world saving animals and campaigning for their rights. They captured the shocking footage of Anne being beaten, which began her journey to freedom, and, when not investigating Europe's last remaining circuses (they claim to have gone undercover in more than twenty), they are flying around the world liberating animals. Their last big project was to free Peru's circus animals.

Jan, a steely but likeable petite woman with a sharp blonde bob, is the boss, while her husband Tim, a serious, grey-haired man, is campaigns director. They are an interesting double-act and were both involved in animal rights campaigning when they met. Despite their work saving various exotic creatures around the world, what brought them together was something far more domestic. Jan was looking for a trap to catch a feral cat and get it spayed and Tim just happened to have one handy. The rest is history and they formed ADI in 1990. Speaking to me from their impressive office on the 26th floor of Millbank Tower, overlooking the Thames and with a front page of the *Daily Mail* from their Mary Chipperfield exposé taking pride of place, they explained their role in Anne's rescue.

Anne first came to their attention in 1995 when they surveyed her winter quarters at the Robertses' circus in Polebrook, Northamptonshire. They tried unsuccessfully for a number of years to sneak someone into the circus – their most successful method of exposing cruelty in circuses – but had no luck. Finally, in January 2011, one of their investigators managed to sneak up to her barn in the dead of night and find a hole to push a camera through from outside, they say. The angle wasn't perfect as she had her back to the camera and neither was the height, but after fifteen years, it was the closest they had come to a breakthrough. They knew that every moment mattered as the majestic animal was fast approaching the end of her days. She had become less and less useful to the circus as the years passed and her arthritis prevented her from performing any tricks or even posing for photos in the ring. For the first time, she was not going on tour with the circus. So with the secret camera installed, they began filming.

The footage they captured shocked even them. There were countless recordings of Nitu hitting and abusing Anne. In total, over just a three-week period, she was hit, punched and walloped with a broom forty-eight times. During some of the assaults, she was stabbed in the face with a pitchfork and smashed around the head with metal and wooden staves. At various stages during these attacks, her arthritic-ridden legs gave way and she nearly fell to her knees. At one point, she tried to flee the blows but the chains – one on her front leg and another on the opposite back leg – kept her shackled in place. The hidden camera also captured the abuse of other animals, including a camel, miniature ponies and horses at the barn.

ADI knew that they had to move quickly to prevent further abuse but also knew that they must ensure they had the footage they needed to go public and to get conviction. 'We knew we only had one shot and it had to work,' Tim says. They told me that one hit is not enough to secure a conviction: you have to establish a pattern of behaviour, and added that they had learned this the hard way in previous failed prosecutions. So to save Anne, they needed to make sure they had enough of the right kind of evidence.

Interestingly, their very first operation together was to investigate Anne's life at the circus, at a time when it had three elephants. 'We took our first footage and photos in about 1995 or 1996,' says Jan. At the time, she was in the winter quarters, living with two other elephants, Beverly and Janie.

ADI's method is to send undercover investigators posing as workers to the circus, where they attempt to capture footage of abuse taking place. This method is, clearly, one entirely reliant on luck: on the circus hiring at the time, on the investigator being chosen, and on them actually gaining access to places where abuse is taking place and being in the right place when it happens. Jan explains: 'We started trying to get people in every season. They would apply for a job at different circuses. But it's a matter of luck if you go to a circus and there is a vacancy and you've got someone who's liked and who's taken on. Then you're away.' But ADI were unable to get anyone into Bobby Roberts Super Circus and so nothing much happened for about five years.

Meanwhile, they had been busy with another undercover operation: infiltrating Mary Chipperfield

Promotions Ltd. At the time, Mary Chipperfield's company supplied animals to organisations across the world including Disney, for whom they provided animals for the film *101 Dalmatians*. Over three months between October 1997 and January 1998, ADI's undercover investigators recorded Chipperfield, a member of the 300-year-old circus dynasty, beating an eighteen-month-old chimpanzee called Trudy with a riding crop. Her then sixty-four-year-old husband Roger Cawley was filmed whipping a sick elephant round a circus ring. Worst of all, farm worker Steve Gills was captured on tape beating elephants with an iron bar, a shovel, a broom and a pitchfork.

In 1999, Chipperfield and Cawley were charged with animal cruelty and appeared at Aldershot Magistrates' Court in Hampshire. They were fined £8,500 for cruelty to animals and ordered to pay costs of £12,240. Chipperfield, then sixty-one, claimed that chimpanzees were 'tough' and would not have been harmed by the violence. She claimed Trudy had tried to bite her and so she had beaten her with a riding crop. But animal experts said the chimp was kept in an 'utterly inappropriate fashion' and had lived in a climate of 'fear and despair'. Gills, who it emerged had killed a woman previously, was jailed for four months for cruelty towards the four elephants. At the time, Jan said that she was disappointed that the couple had not been banned from keeping animals and had only received a small fine. She said: 'This kind of punishment doesn't fit the crime. This was a paltry fine.' Trudy was rehomed at the Monkey World sanctuary in Wareham, Dorset.

Jan said, 'Bobby was on our radar from the beginning of the nineties just like everybody else and really when you're doing undercover work you generally get in where you can get in. We actually tried multiple times to get someone inside Bobby Roberts' after 1996 without success but it's the luck of the draw.'

'That's probably when we started stepping it up and following and so on,' says Tim, 'but we still couldn't get a break. Then Jan said: "We have to film inside the winter quarters," and we brought in our undercover team. We told them they had to get a camera in. We got the amazing footage inside Mary Chipperfield's winter quarters in 1997–8, we got the tent camera in the Great British Circus. It's consistent, this violence to elephants – it's not just a few bad apples. It's everywhere we go.' So ADI had a plan – now it was just a matter of getting in.

They started keeping a close eye on Anne and her companions and began sending undercover investigators round the country following the three elephants while they were on the road with the circus. 'We monitored them really thoroughly,' Tim says. 'So we did timed journeys, we timed her into the container and out again. Given that this elephant was really, really sick, it was disgusting how she was being treated because she was stuck in the transporter for hours and hours and they didn't bother to let her out. That was their normal practice.' He adds: 'I remember we once trailed them from Glasgow down to Polebrook. They had taken all three of the elephants to an event over Christmas and they all pulled into a services really close to Polebrook, checked in to a hotel overnight and just left all the elephants – all three of them – in the transporters all night. They're like coffins on wheels, those things.'

The evidence they claimed to have of Anne's long journeys in a cramped trailer was sadly not enough to secure an animal cruelty conviction, because circus animals were excluded from legislation to protect livestock and zoo animals. 'But there's a reason there's an eight-hour journey limit for livestock in Europe,' explains Tim. 'It's because travelling in transporters is not nice for animals and especially for elephants who are chained because they're pretty much immobilised as otherwise they'll tip the trucks over. So they were just left overnight and then they got up in the morning and moved on again. It's an epic journey from Scotland anyhow and you should break it up, walk the animals, put them back in again, not just think of your own comfort. But once she was really, really ill it was just business as usual, just the same old tour. She should have been taken off, she should never have gone on the tour. Those are the things that sum up Bobby Roberts' husbandry.'

Tim and Jan were truly worried by what happened next. 'I think it was during the winter of 2000 and 2001 that

Beverly and Janie suddenly died and no one knew what had happened to them,' says Jan. 'Basically they went into the winter quarters at the end of the year and didn't come out again the next and there was no investigation. No one knew where the bodies were buried and no one knew what happened to them. There was never any explanation and from that time Anne was alone.' Then in 2002, the group started receiving reports that Anne was sick. 'She had become absolutely skeletal, she lost so much weight,' Jan says. 'We even sent wildlife advisor Simon Adams there to speak to Bobby to ask if we could do anything. In the end, it didn't come to anything. He wouldn't use our vet and he got in touch with his own, who wouldn't consult with ours but she did eventually start to recover.' They still don't know what was wrong with her but suspect her arthritis had something to do with it. Jan adds: 'There was always an ongoing argument with Bobby about giving her arthritis medicine. He kept saying that she wouldn't take it but the point is that if you've got an animal that's in pain, I think you can hide it in her food or something.'

Eventually, in 2011, their investigator managed to sneak a camera into the barn. It wasn't at the right angle and Anne partially obscured the view. Also, they had wanted two cameras to ensure that they had a good view of the situation, but they couldn't get another one in. But it was the furthest they'd got and they had to give it a go. Tim says: 'When we got the first still back, we thought she'd just stand in front of the camera and we wouldn't see anything. We said: "We must try and find another angle." It was a big barn, you find gaps, but we couldn't. We had to go with the one shot and let it record from one position.'

When they watched the footage, they were horrified by the pain and suffering that was being meted out to Anne on a daily basis. There was a 'stunning' amount of violence, according to Tim, but it wasn't just her that suffered. Nitu can be seen beating and thumping ponies, kicking a camel and spitting in its face.

Describing her thoughts on seeing the video for the first time, Jan says: 'For us, obviously, we don't enjoy looking at animal cruelty. Nobody does. But the real feeling for us is: "Have we got it? Do we have what looks like a conviction here? Is there enough? Is it strong enough?" And for Tim and I really, that's the key thing that goes through our minds even though we're looking at it and thinking how horrific it is.' She adds: 'My heart went out to Anne. Sometimes you look at these large powerful animals and you think: "Just do something, just fight back, just stand up for yourself." But the other side of that is: "Well, OK, now it can stop. We've got you on film, we've got enough and now it can stop."'

As many of the animal welfare groups involved in Anne's story have said, it was actually not the violence towards her that was the worst thing, it was her pitiful existence. 'The first stuff we saw was her chained in the barn,' Tim explains, 'and I remember thinking what a bloody dreadful life. I just thought how empty must this dingy, completely immobilised, horrible, horrible, squalid existence be. And to just go in and look at that and not think there's a problem with that. Then, when the violence began to unfold, I just remember thinking: "Bloody hell, this is a very, very nasty place." You could immediately see that the violence was really casual because I've seen workers before who glance around and they're slightly wary and they're doing little sly punches, but this was like: "I don't care if Bobby walks through the door, I'm swinging at this elephant."'

'Her life was wretched, absolutely wretched,' says Jan. 'And you can tell by looking at the attacks after a number of hours that it's nothing to do with anything the animals are doing, it's just this person enjoying whatever it is, whatever satisfaction they get from being violent. You can tell it's something coming from them like a release or something and the animal is just a victim. It's just in the wrong place at the wrong time and it can't do anything to protect itself. And you've got a person there who wants to do things like that to it and there are so many of them. It's just so wretched and so disgusting.'

Another harrowing moment for the couple to see was when Bobby walked into the shed. As Anne reached out her trunk to him, he kicked it away. 'I remember when Bobby came in,' says Tim, 'and he's in a suit and you think he's been on a day out or something or other and he's just stood there with his hands in his pockets and there is no empathy for this animal that he's put in chains, there's just no bond or anything and you can see it. And you just think: "You put her in that horrific bondage and then you just walk off and have your tea." That sums up how these animals are broken as well and what an awful life they lead because the one person she seeks succour from, some sort of comfort and solace, is the person who did it to her. It's Stockholm Syndrome. That to me is one of the most wretched scenes in all the footage.'

Jan says she also struggled with the scene. 'When she reaches out to him and she's lived with him all her life, he's all she's ever known and her companions have died, he hits her and rejects her. I just couldn't understand. I couldn't see how he could respond to these animals which are so emotional, so intelligent... they have culture, they communicate, they mourn their dead, and he gets nothing. You can see there is nothing there for him.'

ADI were criticised for sitting on the footage by the judge during the Robertses' trial but Tim responds acidly: 'We were criticised that we left it so long to get it published but everyone else let it happen for twenty-five years.' Jan explains that the reason for the delay was the need to make a time-coded index of every piece of footage, which usually takes three times as long as the actual recording. She also says that they had to bring in more staff to deal with the burden – and they knew that they had to get it perfect because previously they had learned the hard way that it takes a lot to get an animal cruelty conviction. 'We learned during our very first prosecutions that one hit is not enough,' she says. 'Even a couple of hits are not enough in order to pursue a conviction. You have to show that it's a pattern of behaviour and so you have to show multiple hits. It's surprising how much abuse you have to show towards an animal to get an actual conviction.' She adds: 'Our obsession with evidence is born of experience. It's from the first few times we filmed beatings and nothing could be done about it because we didn't have enough and the person had an excuse. We learned from that and we knew we had to be absolutely thorough and we had to get it nailed.'

So Tim and Jan started sifting through the footage and compiled enough for a prosecution and a news story. The more they watched, the more they realised they were sitting on a very big exposé and so they drafted in extra help to get through all the material. Working non-stop for weeks, they say they watched every piece of footage three times, noting who went in, who went out, in time-coded sequences, and what was happening in great detail. Then they watched everything again to work out what the excuses would be, they say.

'What we're looking for is: are there any circumstances

that would make this happen?' Tim says. 'Has the elephant surged at the guy ten minutes earlier? They always say the animal tried to attack them.'

'We try to work out what their excuse will be,' adds Jan. 'You'd be surprised at the excuses.'

They would also have to identify those committing the abuse: often difficult on grainy footage and when the workers wear different outfits every day and are recruited on a casual basis. 'You know when workers are involved,' says Tim, 'that the odds are they're going to disappear the moment you put it out.'

Then, finally, a decision had to be made about whether they went ahead with releasing the footage with a view to a prosecution. 'We get to a point with these investigations,' explains Tim, 'and we have to make a decision, which is: "If we stop now, then that's it. There's no other chance. We'll never get it again." It's like putting everything on a number in roulette. There are clearly things which, I think, if this investigation had run longer – if we'd had a bigger window, say – then we probably would have got more. We'd have probably got more definitive evidence on all of the other animals.'

ADI were also criticised during the court case for not bringing the footage to the attention of the police or the RSPCA immediately. But their argument is that, had they done so, there would never have been a public outcry and there would never have been an incentive to move Anne quickly. They say it was also likely that the groom would have fled and that the authorities would have put the saga down to a rogue employee. This would have meant that there was a very real danger that Anne might have been left at the circus – something ADI wanted to prevent at all costs.

The organisation was also accused of having fabricated the footage during the trial – something they vehemently deny. RSPCA inspector Jody Gordon recalls that the video ADI produced was very similar to a video they made of alleged cruelty towards elephants at the Great British Circus. He also noted the parallels – the men in question both wore caps and disappeared as soon as the footage was about to be released. He says that from his examination of the winter quarters, he did not think anyone had climbed under the fence to plant a camera as ADI said they did. ADI deny that they faked the footage and the judge at the Robertses' trial accepted this.

The judge also told them that they had prolonged Anne's suffering by sitting on the footage for weeks before releasing it. But ADI remains unapologetic. 'Can you imagine how long it takes you to write down notes on three weeks of footage?' says Jan. 'If you watch ten minutes, it's a minimum of thirty minutes to go through it because you have to watch it three times, work out what's going on and then write it down. And we had a whole team of people watching the footage and then writing it down and someone checking what they were writing. Because it was going to court it had to be absolutely correct. The police couldn't do it. It had to be done by people who knew what was going on.' Tim adds: 'You're putting together a legal case, something that's going to make the government understand all of those factors. Otherwise, they just get away with it.'

So the couple formulated a plan to release the footage to the media. And they chose to give it to the *Daily Mail*, not only one of Britain's best-selling and most influential newspapers, but, most importantly, one that is read by animal lovers. Having covered the Mary Chipperfield story exclusively, the *Mail* had a good relationship with ADI. But the judge also criticised ADI for passing the footage to the media first, and not to the police or the Crown Prosecution Service (CPS), which is responsible for bringing prosecutions, or to the RSPCA. 'Ultimately, it's the press coverage that got her out,' is Tim's explanation. 'If we'd presented it to the CPS, it would have taken more than a year for a prosecution and they'd likely have not confiscated the elephant.' Jan adds: 'I said to the [police and the CPS] that the media had more chance of getting Anne out quickly than they did. In our experience if we need an animal rescued quickly, the media does it for us every time. It's sad and I'm sure it's frustrating for the police and the CPS – they want to keep everything to themselves and do it all very carefully and wait a year.

But the animal is still there while they're doing that unless the media steps in.' She adds that relying on the police and the CPS was also a risk: 'Because if you go ahead and the prosecution gets it wrong, the animal may never get out.'

Many would agree with them that using the media was an effective method. Within hours of the story appearing in the newspaper, there was a huge public backlash and calls from all sections of society, from celebrity campaigners to Facebook petitioners, to deliver Anne from her miserable existence. This pressure mounted following the relentless coverage in the *Mail* and every other newspaper and broadcaster that had picked up the story.

Eventually, the Robertses agreed to give Anne up. A number of sanctuaries, zoos and safari parks offered to rehome her in the lap of luxury now she was a national celebrity. And when the CPS agreed to take over ADI's public prosecution, they said that it was because of the 'overwhelming public interest' that the case had generated. So, while ADI hadn't followed the procedure the judge would have preferred, they secured a huge coup in saving Anne, rehoming her and giving her a better life, as well as saving Monty the camel, who was also rehomed, and securing animal cruelty convictions. The publicity surrounding the story reignited the campaign for banning wild animals in circuses and there is no doubt that the widespread coverage helped galvanise public opinion and made a ban more likely. It was, without doubt, a thumping victory.

For ADI, the story was never just about Anne – it was about the use of all wild animals in circuses. The judge at the Robertses' trial accused the organization of having an 'agenda'. The release of the footage came as Parliamentary debate raged around whether to ban wild animals in circuses. At the time, Jan said of Anne's rescue: 'This is a wonderful day and it is also time to say never again and end the use of wild animals in circuses. Today is a day to celebrate, but not relax. It is vital that Defra [the Department for Environment, Food & Rural Affairs] finally implements its promise to ban the use of wild animals in circuses. Let's learn the lesson and ensure that there can never be suffering like this again in the UK.' She stressed that there was 'overwhelming public support' for a ban but 'nothing to stop any British circus from bringing in another elephant tomorrow to replace Anne and the tragic cycle starts again'.

Reflecting on the operation, Tim says: 'It was a very hard undercover. We're probably the only people who could have pulled it off. No one else does anything like that and we've pulled it off on several occasions. It took many, many goes.' But he says he still isn't satisfied with how it played out: 'It's sometimes very frustrating for us because we know all these things and we're trying to persuade the prosecutors. For us, the most frustrating thing was that she had moved into the barn in November 2010 and so although our footage was from January to February, she had actually been in that same position since the previous November. And I think for changing things for animals people needed to know that but we got it in as quickly as we could as it was difficult to set up.'

ADI say that the operation cost them £140,000 and they ended the year in deficit, but it was money 'well spent', according to Jan: 'The reason we exist is to save animals and we don't get it back, but we saved her. It's the same with Bolivia. Bolivia was £1.2m but we emptied a country of its circus animals and we got twenty-five lions to a good home. Same with Peru and it's going to be Colombia now. That's thirty-three lions, a bear, a tiger and about eighty monkeys. That's what we're here for and as long as we're getting them out, we're happy.'

CHAPTER 3

THE MOVE TO LONGLEAT

As soon as Anne's story broke, a huge problem presented itself: how to get her out of the circus and to safety. The first difficulty was persuading the Robertses to let her go. She had lived with them since childhood and had never known anything else. Also, previous attempts to persuade them to give her up had ended in stalemate. And once that huge problem was overcome there was the further issue of where on earth she would go. As Jon Cracknell, director of animal operations at Longleat, where Anne now lives, points out: if you have an abused dog to rehome, there are thousands of kennels to send them to, but where do you put an elephant?

Although it seemed sensible to move her to a zoo with an existing herd of elephants, in reality, this was hugely problematic. Anne was more used to the company of humans than other elephants, having lived in the circus all her life. She had lost her two elephant companions more than a decade earlier. Introducing her to an existing herd was a risky strategy. Elephant herds are matriarchal, meaning mothers, grandmothers, daughters and aunts tend to stick together. Anne would likely struggle as she would have no link to any of the elephants in the herd. Introducing new elephants to established herds is also rather like introducing a child to a class at school late in the year: a possible recipe for disaster. Given her age and health and Bobby's insistence that she didn't get on with other elephants, it was always going to be a difficult decision. More difficult still is the reality that if the herd didn't like her and there was a battle for dominance, she would probably be the loser. You cannot come between two elephants having a fight.

And so an intensive behind-the-scenes operation began to decide what to do next. One of those who picked up the *Daily Mail* and read the story when it broke that Saturday was Jon Cracknell, who had accepted the job but not yet started at Longleat. A trained vet, with six years' experience working with elephants, and an elephant advisor to the British and Irish Association of Zoos and Aquariums (BIAZA), he began to wonder whether his future employers could offer her a home. An animal obsessive who had wanted to be a vet since the age of nine, he specialised in anaesthesia, especially in elephants and bears. As he wandered around the Lanes in Brighton that day, following a party the night before, he phoned his soon-to-be boss David Bradley, who he knew wanted elephants at Longleat. 'I'm not keen on elephants in captivity,' Jon says. 'I don't think I have the ability and the facilities... but Longleat does have a lot of space and potential and in this case it was fairly unique in that here was an elephant that needed a home. So whilst I wasn't actively looking for elephants, there was an interest from Longleat because it was felt that the safari park should have elephants. Anne came along and with my strong background in welfare – having worked for several organisations globally – I just felt, right, we can do something which a lot of other places can't.'

At the time, Anne was an old lady and hadn't been expected to live that long, so Jon thought Longleat could offer her a temporary home. His initial dilemma was how to contact the Robertses. The circus was on the road and he feared any letter he sent would get lost among the hate mail. Plus, time was of the essence – Anne urgently needed to be found a new home. So Jon contacted a vet he knew who had worked in circuses, and who luckily happened to know the couple, and sent them Jon's number. The next day – Sunday – Moira

Roberts made contact. 'Moira rang me up,' says Jon, 'and said: "Is there anything you can do to help us?" because she was having such a terrible time. She said they'd been looking for a new home for Anne for ten years but discussions with animal charities hadn't come to anything.'

The ball had started rolling. And it turned out that others had also thought of Longleat. Matt Ford, owner of Specialist Wildlife Services (SWS), an animal rescue company that rehomes exotic animals for zoos and governments, had also seen the newspaper coverage of Anne. He had independently come to the conclusion that Longleat would be a good spot as it had previously been home to an elephant herd a decade ago and still had an elephant house. With Matt's expertise in logistics and moving animals, Jon's work as a vet with knowledge of elephant welfare and Longleat as a potential base, they had the beginnings of a plan... and not a moment too soon. As the operation to get Anne out of the circus gathered pace, the public outcry was growing and the story was being carried daily via every major newspaper and media outlet, both in Britain and internationally. Subjected to a huge backlash, the Robertses were panicking. Recalling his experience of meeting them, Jon says: 'They told me they had grief and petitioning outside the circus. They'd had people outside slagging them off, they'd had phone calls and verbal abuse personally.'

Pressure was also being applied behind the scenes. RSPCA inspector Jody Gordon, who was with the charity's Special Operations Unit which handles investigations, had noted the fallout and spoke to Bobby privately about his options. 'I spoke to Bobby and said: "Look with everything that's gone on with Anne's health as it is now, I think this is probably going to be the time where you're going to need to sign her over and find her a new home, because if you don't the pressure will come on for an investigation against you anyway. Beyond that, even if there's no investigation, I don't think that you will be able to travel with Anne without coming under severe public pressure."'

On the Tuesday morning, Jon met with the Robertses in Cheshire, where the circus was camped at the time. 'I sat with them for about an hour and they told me what a shit time they were having,' he says. 'They were lovely, actually. They were really welcoming and they weren't suspicious. Well, they were a little bit suspicious because they didn't know me and that's fair enough. We had a big chat and basically we agreed that Longleat could offer her a home and they were happy with it and that was that.'

Though it was, of course, slightly more complicated than that. Jon, mindful of the fact that there could be a conflict of interest if Longleat owned Anne, agreed with the Robertses that ownership of Anne should go to SWS. 'We don't own her – we never owned her. I'm not stupid,' he says. 'The idea is I'm looking out for Anne's welfare so we maintain and look after her but we don't actually own her.' He is very insistent on the point that no money changed hands between Longleat and the Robertses. Matt Ford of SWS also states that there was no financial arrangement and no guarantee or otherwise given to the Robertses. Neither he nor Jon has an ongoing relationship with the couple, they say. So Matt took over ownership and the planning could begin.

But there was another much more pressing issue than simply removing Anne from the circus. The RSPCA had visited to review her health on the Tuesday after the footage emerged. Tim Bouts, head vet at Whipsnade at the time, who is experienced in working with elephants, wrote the report. In it, he noted his concern about her health. He also said he was concerned that she had no regular access to water, though Bobby said it was regularly given to her directly rather than left out for her to drink. He wrote: 'Lameness due to arthritis seems to be so severe that transport of the animal would not currently be safe and could well be in contravention of legislation on animal transportation.'

He tells me: 'I could see she had very bad arthritis and I said we should immediately start treating it. I said if the treatment didn't work that euthanasia was an option because she was an elderly animal who was in pain constantly.' This was a huge dilemma: risk moving

Anne and possibly compromise her welfare, or leave her at the circus, where her welfare was already not good. Worryingly, his report concluded: 'Ultimately, if the arthritis cannot be satisfactorily controlled to allow safe transport and the welfare of the elephant is too compromised, then euthanasia would be considered a valid option in a case like this.' They were the words no one had wanted to hear.

The *Daily Mail*, which had already started receiving letters from readers wanting to pledge money to Anne's future happiness, had to issue a warning about her health and explain why it couldn't accept donations towards her future. Jon Cracknell says: 'I don't think you'd have had any problems euthanising her as she was. Actually, you could justify it. Euthanasia can solve a complex issue sometimes and I think the recommendation was justifiable because at that time there was nowhere for her to go but it was felt that she should be given a chance to see if we could help.'

The following day, Nic Masters, then an independent vet and now head of veterinary services at the Zoological Society of London (ZSL), assessed Anne. Nic – also chair of the UK Elephant Welfare Group (EWG) – says he was 'shocked' by her appearance and how 'ragged' she was, but decided it was in her interests to go ahead with the move. 'I got to see her on some pain relief, already much improved, and I think I still thought long and hard about whether it was OK to move her,' he explains. He didn't think, however, it was viable to send her to an overseas sanctuary. 'I remember thinking very early on that that seemed like completely the wrong idea. I thought that transport in the UK was probably going to be acceptable but anything more would be too much for her, certainly at that time. I was worried that she wouldn't be able to stay upright, to be honest. I was worried from a physical point of view that if she went down on the plane, for example, and was unable to get up again, what on earth people would do, how awful would that be.'

'There were risks,' says Jon, 'there are always risks with moving any animal – but they were more so for Anne. But the benefits of moving her and getting her out of her current situation outweighed the risk of leaving her. So there was no benefit to not moving her.'

Things were now moving at a rapid pace. Wednesday saw the first planning meeting at the RSPCA headquarters in Horsham, West Sussex. Previously, the RSPCA had discussed moving Anne with the Robertses. The charity's Dr Ros Clubb acknowledges that the Robertses were receptive, but says that a suitable new home could not be found for her, and so she remained. Longleat, she says, didn't appear on the radar as they hadn't had elephants for at least a decade: 'It was only when the ADI footage of her being beaten emerged that obviously everything stepped up. That was when Longleat came forward to say we've got these old facilities and guys on site who used to manage these elephants.' She concludes it was the 'ideal scenario' for an 'emergency exit' for Anne, though concedes it wasn't perfect long-term because it wasn't large and had resident rhinos.

Jon Cracknell and Matt Ford decided to bring lots of organisations to the table in a kind of wildlife welfare summit to decide what was best for Anne's future. In attendance at the top-secret meeting were Jon, Matt, Nic Masters, the RSPCA, the Born Free Foundation – which campaigns to keep wildlife in the wild – and ADI, who had shot the footage. But it wasn't long before the first difficulties began.

ADI had been monitoring Anne since the mid-nineties and took a great interest in her welfare. When they finally secured the footage to get her out of the circus, they were understandably keen to be involved in the next stage but their fundamental aims as an animal rights group fighting to keep animals in the wild were, like Born Free's, at odds with Longleat's, a safari park which was home to numerous captive wild animals on show to the public. ADI wanted Anne to be taken to an elephant sanctuary in the US, where she could live out her days with other elephants in something akin to her natural habitat. Others had read the veterinary reports and were seriously concerned about her health and were still considering euthanasia. It was to prove a difficult point – Jon describes it as a 'fairly heated debate' – and the meeting apparently ended with an RSPCA lawyer storming out of the room. Luckily, there was consensus on the point that Anne needed to be moved to a place of safety as quickly as possible and so it was agreed by everyone that she would go to Longleat. A press release was then issued.

So a team was assembled and the planning entered its final stages. Matt took over logistics. He knew where to get an elephant truck – not a small feat to track down in a country with not many elephants. There were actually two trucks in the UK, but one was Bobby's and it had 'Bobby Roberts Super Circus' emblazoned on the side. The prospect of moving Anne in that, with animal rights protesters on the lookout, was not a good one. As Jon says: 'We didn't know what to expect. There was so much antagonism at the time. You couldn't be in a Bobby Roberts van – you'd have got stopped and she'd have suffered.' So instead, Matt approached Woburn, who had an elephant truck. Unfortunately, they hadn't used it for a long time. 'Now the first challenge was on the first day,' says Jon, 'because the Woburn van hadn't been used and hadn't moved elephants in a long while. Because of this, it hadn't had its MOT and it wasn't roadworthy. So we looked, and the nearest appointment we could get for the vehicle was something like in three or four weeks. I was like: "Crap! What are we going to do?"' But luckily, the RSPCA phoned a contact in the Department for Transport, who pulled some strings, and the van was approved the following afternoon. Without that intervention, the operation could have been very seriously delayed.

So the team was now ready to go. It included John Minion from Yorkshire Wildlife Park, an ex-elephant keeper who had experience in moving elephants, Lynne Thomson, who was head of elephants at Woburn, cameramen from SWS, who were to document the whole thing, the Born Free Foundation and the RSPCA as observers, and Jon and Nic Masters on hand for veterinary support.

Meanwhile, Longleat had to be prepared for Anne's imminent arrival. The elephant house had been converted into a rhino house after Longleat's herd of elephants moved out, so they had to get metal workers in to set about making it once again suitable for elephants. Although the original framework remained, since the rhinos had moved in everything had been converted and downsized. Extra posts had been put in, which all needed to be removed, the doors had to be beefed up so she couldn't pull them off with her three-tonne frame and hay mangers needed to be installed. It was a daunting task.

On the Saturday night, the team assembled for the move. Although it had been confirmed that Anne would go to Longleat, no one knew when it would happen and the mission was carried out in great secrecy. I was one of the few people who knew it was going ahead because Longleat had agreed to work with the *Daily Mail* newspaper after we exposed what had happened. The team stayed at Lynne Thomson's house that night, ready to depart in the dark early hours of Sunday morning on the mission, which cost £15,000.

They arrived at Polebrook, the winter quarters of the circus, a few hours later as day was breaking. This was when the hard work started and everyone was nervous. As Chris Draper of the Born Free Foundation put it: 'The mind boggled at the potential of how badly wrong it could go.' They were worried about what the industry calls 'antis' – animal rights protesters – attacking the site after police had warned them that this could occur. Protesters were now picketing the circus every day and the internet was abuzz with threats against the Robertses, while newspapers and television news carried daily updates on Anne's plight. For this reason, police oversaw the move. Extraordinarily, they put Anne in the same category as a high security prisoner, so she could only be mentioned on the police radio waves using a code name. As a Category A prisoner, she had a police escort out of Polebrook and a police escort at the other end to ensure the move was safe and stress-free.

When they arrived at the barn, it was the first time many of the members of the team had seen Anne since the abuse. Chris Draper of the Born Free Foundation says: 'I'd seen her several times in the preceding years on the road and I'd always been very concerned about her gait in particular. It hadn't changed much; it was still the same. She was dragging her feet but that implies to me it was obviously arthritis. She wasn't a mobile animal and needed proper care for it rather than to be loaded into a van each week and be shipped off here, there and everywhere.' He says that her condition was 'pretty crummy' when he arrived, and adds: 'I think she'd improved from when the first inspection had happened because they'd got her on some pain medication by then so she seemed alert and bright but her skin was terrible – really, really bad. One of her ears was just covered in dead skin. She obviously hadn't been given access to anything to scratch upon. Her feet looked a bit of a mess – there were one or two lumps and bumps on her. You could obviously see the gait issue was never going away. She didn't look good.'

So without further hesitation, it was time to load Anne and get her away from the circus forever. There had been much discussion of how exactly to get her on to the truck. Everyone agreed that it needed to be done with the utmost care as lots could go wrong but in the event, the reins were handed to Bobby. Jon recalls him simply saying to her: 'Come on' and her plodding straight into the truck. But Chris Draper says it was slightly more complicated. 'If I remember rightly, they needed Bobby to walk her in as that was the simplest and safest thing,' he says. 'I think he lost his temper a little bit but he managed to get her in there. He was tugging on her trunk a few times – it wasn't quite as smooth as I'd imagine he wanted it to be – but she got in and it was fairly stress-free, I have to say. She's done it a million times, hasn't she? She's got into trucks and out of trucks so in theory it shouldn't have been a problem. She was loaded up uneventfully and we were on our way.'

With a police escort on to the motorway, the team left for Longleat in convoy with Bobby and their precious cargo. The five-hour move was tense: the elephant truck had video and they could see her discomfort. Jon says that because of Anne's difficulty in standing, there was a worry she could fall because of the swaying movement on the journey. 'She wasn't very happy, but we took it slowly,' he explains. 'She had trouble with the move. She's moved a lot herself but with her orthopaedic issues there were concerns that she might go down and you have to plan for everything. So if she went down or was ill, we had a team there for euthanasia because, to be honest, it was a bit of a risk moving her and we weren't sure if she could be moved. So we took a bit of a chance with that but we felt it was the right thing to do to get her to a better place.'

They had planned the journey carefully, but it wasn't all smooth running. The police had advised them to go via Bath, from where they would have an escort to Longleat. Jon simply says it wasn't 'ideal'. He adds: 'No one realised that an elephant was going past. It's amazing. Even though the truck had "Woburn elephants" down the side of it, no one even noticed.'

Eventually, on Sunday afternoon, they arrived at Longleat. It had been a huge race against time to finish Anne's enclosure before her arrival, and in the event she was about half an hour early so the truck had to be parked up in the woods while the welding was finished and everything was given a last check and clean-up. Again, they had the dilemma of how to get her off the truck and this time it was more complex. Longleat is a huge safari park that hosts more than a million visitors a year. The team felt that no chances could be taken with her safety – and everyone else's.

It was decided that she should be taken into the enclosure using chains. This meant shackling her ankles in chains and then walking her in, one step at a time. Bobby could not comprehend why they wouldn't let him walk her in, while the Born Free Foundation were not happy at all but the chaining went ahead. Jon says: 'We insisted on the chains to move her because she was unpredictable and we didn't know what would happen. She was chained from a safety point of view. To be fair to Bobby, he wasn't actually very happy with that because he felt he could have just walked her in and he could've done, but in retrospect if she'd charged off on a rampage and killed a load of people and we had to shoot her that would be pretty disastrous – and you have to consider that. You've got to remember that this is one week after the newspaper article and an elephant move is usually planned a year in advance.' He concludes: 'It wasn't compromising her welfare just for that two minutes to walk in.'

Anne's former keeper Ryan Hockley, who is now head of safari at the park and who had experience with Longleat's last herd of elephants, which went to France in 2001, recalls: 'There was quite a lot of hullabaloo when she moved in, with people looking nervous. When elephants are loading or unloading, it's nerve-wracking. We always have to plan so it's safe. In the world we live in now you're nice to elephants. We do give them a lot of respect and assume that if you give them an opportunity to show their distress in a stressful situation, they will take it.' He also admits that there were fears when she first arrived that she would be 'damaged goods', but adds: 'All we knew is she had to get out of where she was and come here to an alternative home.'

So on that Sunday, 3 April 2011, Anne finally arrived at her retirement home. And, like any pensioner after a long journey, she was exhausted. 'I think she was tired,' Jon says. 'It was a long journey. It's a long journey for anyone, and she's in her old age and she's knackered and she had to stand and everything else.' But what happened next surprised everyone. With the zeal of a toddler in a particularly foul tantrum, Anne lay waste to her enclosure, which had been so lovingly prepared for her. Perhaps she'd realised she was finally free, perhaps it was just her way of saying thank you, but she tore her new habitat to bits when she arrived.

'Suddenly she had an area where she could do what she wanted,' says Jon. 'You can read into it what you like, that she's so suppressed, but she went out there and she was chucking stuff and she basically broke everything she could and she smashed it. She cut her trunk up – she was an arse!'

But she was free. She had a new home, which she shared with five rhinos, a paddock to herself to run free in and a lovely view of some ponds with pelicans and flamingos and the sweeping, Capability Brown-designed landscape of Longleat Safari Park & Adventure Park.

A new chapter was beginning.

CHAPTER 4

ANNE'S NEW LIFE AT LONGLEAT AND PLANS FOR A SANCTUARY

Larking about in her sand pit and tearing into an already-battered tree trunk, Anne the elephant looked most content with her new life at Longleat. I could hardly believe my eyes. Last time I had seen her, she had ambled slowly but purposefully towards me, dragging her hind legs, and now she was scurrying about like a toddler. It was an unbelievable transformation and one you had to see to believe. Now, finally, days on from the end of her suffering, Anne was free to do as she liked and to come and go as she pleased. And she seemed to be taking full advantage of this when I saw her in her new paddock at Longleat. It was a joyful and gratifying sight. I had played a small part in securing this animal's freedom. It was a well-deserved happy ending for Britain's last circus elephant – one that had endured more than most.

So Anne had taken her final bow and said goodbye to the circus and hello to her new retirement home. And, like any old person, she had a few health issues that needed to be seen to. A team of vets and osteopaths descended on the safari park to give her a full health MOT. They carried out blood tests, X-rays of her feet and ultrasounds of her body. An osteopath carried out thermography on her to look at heat patterns to detect pain. As Jon Cracknell puts it: 'Pretty much anything that could be checked was checked.'

Longleat were open to anything that could help her get better, including an acupuncturist – though happily for Anne, they used normal-sized needles rather than elephant-sized ones as they need only pierce the first few layers of skin. Most bizarrely of all, they brought in an elephant whisperer, who used crystals and Reiki on Anne. 'We had Margrit Coates here. She's an animal healer,' Jon says. Heading off the inevitable scepticism, he adds: 'Did she bring anything to it? Well, she didn't do any harm, put it that way! I've seen some interesting things. Animals respond in different ways and the thing about Margrit is that she's really calm and just creates a warm atmosphere, so even if that's the best she was doing, it was still positive for Anne.'

The first major health issue to address was Anne's skin: she was covered in dead skin, which had accumulated because she had had no scratching post and so no way of getting rid of the dead cells. She had large mounds of dark skin attached to her and a dark pallor as a result. The large black rings around her eyes that made her look almost like a panda were a result of the Robertses using oil on her eyes to moisturise the dead skin, Jon says. At Longleat, though, she had a new skincare routine. 'Her skin was what looked worst and it was bad, but we gave her rubbing posts, daily baths and scrubbed her with brushes,' Jon recalls. 'She just leant in and really enjoyed it. That was quite a lot of work to get rid of that dead skin. We used different creams and different preparations to help soften it and improve the skin and now she's just stunning.'

When Anne arrived at Longleat, she found a large tree trunk she could use as a scratching post. 'She was just rubbing and scratching and she was really enjoying herself,' says Jon. 'That big tree trunk, I think that lasted forty-eight hours. She battered that so much and rolled around in the big sand piles. It was just the scratching. I think she was so relieved to scratch because she didn't have any scratching posts or anything.' Unfortunately, though, he continues, she was slightly too enthusiastic and ended up hurting herself: 'She cut her trunk. She was a doofus, actually. Basically she was just lashing into the log and she was enjoying it so much she ended up cutting herself.'

Within days her skin had improved and, in weeks, it was almost as it would have been had she stayed in the wild. Remarkably, as the skin was exfoliated away, it revealed that her ears were actually a bright shade of pink. Although remnants of dead skin remain because the problem was so ingrained, it is probably just 1 per cent of what was there, according to Jon. Already she was looking far better.

The second issue was less easy to deal with. A life of performance and constant touring at the circus, not to mention old age and being chained to the floor, had left Anne with problems in her back legs. She was diagnosed with arthritis in her right hind leg in 2003, but Bobby Roberts had not been giving her suitable pain relief. He claimed she would not take it and insists he followed veterinary advice. So she had been forced to suffer the pain without sufficient medication for years. She was immediately put on pain relief and then given blood and other health tests. 'The biggest challenge that we couldn't fix was her legs,' says Jon. 'But from the point of view of the arthritis, we just had to get her on a good regular pain relief system. The orthopaedic side of things we've got as good as we can. She still drags her legs but if you compare it to what she was like when she was loading, she's much better.' Jon says that they give her glucosamine and cod liver oil supplements to support her joints. 'She dragged her back legs on the ground before she arrived at Longleat, but now she can get an inch's clearance from the ground so there's not as much damage as there was,' he explains.

Asked why he thought she had such serious problems with her legs, Jon explains: 'I think it's from the circus days. Either she might have had an injury or it's just her age and abnormal weight bearing. An elephant's designed to take weight on four legs. If you repeatedly get her walking on two for a matinee and evening performance, and then walking on a ball or a tub, then you're going to change the mechanics of the joints and over time you're going to get arthritis.' He says elephants do rear up on their hind legs in the wild to forage, but it's rare. He also claims that it may be because Anne is the oldest elephant in Europe that we are seeing problems that would happen to all elephants at that age. According to him though, other elephants who are not far behind her in age do not have the same problems, so he puts it down to her life in the circus. To help ease the strain, the team have put her on an exercise programme to build muscle and reduce fat so that the joints are better supported and she weighs less so there is less strain on them. 'When you weigh her, her weight has dropped a little but not hugely, but she was flabby with no muscle,' he says. 'Now she's muscle without fat. She's got muscles supporting the joints so it's not joint on joint,' he adds.

Anne's personal osteopath Tony Nevin treated her previously at the circus, but admits she had gone downhill drastically when he first saw her at Longleat. 'Her condition by then had deteriorated a lot,' he recalls. 'It was a mixture of age and care.' He adds that she'd aged considerably: 'When I first met her she'd interact with you but her eyes had lost their sparkle.' He remembers that by the time she'd left the circus, her posture and muscling and skin condition had deteriorated and she looked a 'mess'.

When I asked Tony how exactly he treated a huge elephant – given it would be difficult to give one a massage – he explained: 'What you're trying to do when treating an elephant is improve circulation and lower the amount of muscle tension. So we do techniques where she's standing and you can lean in and create very gentle stretches for the muscles. We also stimulate little trigger points within the muscles so that you create areas of localised tension. Looking at her move, if she's got good circulation through the muscles then the skin will be loose over them.' He also uses an infrared thermal imaging camera to give an immediate indication of what the blood flow is like under the skin. The treatments he gives Anne every three weeks take about ten minutes and then he stays for an hour or more assessing her. He adds that she has now got the sparkle back in her eyes.

Nic Masters also came in to assess her regularly. 'I was pleasantly surprised by how well she did over time,' he says. 'It just goes to show how important pain relief can be. Animals, just like people that are in chronic pain, get really down. That seemed to make a big difference to her.'

Anne could not raise her trunk higher than her belly when she arrived at Longleat. Jon says there were stories circulating at the time that if an ankus or bullhook, a metal stick used to control an elephant, was used or if they were beaten, they would lose the use of their trunk. He says that he didn't believe them: he simply thought that she had been given her food on the floor and so had not needed to lift it up. 'If you're sitting on the sofa watching daytime telly, you become a big, fat blimp, but also you become weak, your muscles become weak. And I think what was happening was her food was just presented on the floor so she only had to take her trunk to the floor and that was it. There were no real opportunities to explore.'

To address this problem the team positioned her food higher and higher so that she got used to moving her trunk again. They used cranes and winches to suspend food above her and over time her trunk has improved. Now, according to Jon, it's almost as good as it would have been in the wild. And though she occasionally suffers from a few cracked nails and abscesses on her feet, it's nothing the vets can't handle, he says.

Sadly, not all of Anne's scars were visible on her arrival at Longleat. 'Vets can easily fix an elephant physically, but mentally, it's a different matter,' Jon told the *Daily Mail* at the time. 'We believe Anne was possibly suffering the animal equivalent of post-traumatic stress disorder when she arrived. But because we knew very little about her history – only what we were told by Bobby Roberts, plus a few photographs and a couple of videos – it was difficult for us to know what specifically we needed to do to help her.' He says that he had very little insight into her past and her behaviour, so the team have had to learn as they go along.

Anne's psychological scars manifested themselves in her physical behaviour and she still sways from side-to-side – something animal behaviourists call stereotyping. At first her keepers thought it would gradually fade away once she got used to her new home, but it hasn't and she still does it today. Elephant expert Khyne U Mar says that Anne would not now be able to stop the repetitive behaviour she developed at the circus: 'Once elephants develop stereotypic behaviour at any point in their lifetime it's very, very difficult to get rid of. It's incurable. All you can do to reduce this behaviour is to make them busy or do something interesting – we call this "enrichment" – or if there is no companion elephant, somebody should talk to her and be with her. She needs exercise and she needs a changing environment.'

Anne's first keeper at Longleat was Andy Hayton, who has since left the park. He worked with Longleat's original herd of elephants and was there when the Chipperfields were involved with it. Her new home boasted views of ponds full of pelicans and flamingos and she shared a house with a group of rhinos and the park with lions, which roam the woods behind the compound.

Andy told the *Mail* at the time that she was happy at the safari park though she was scared of the pelicans, who she 'absolutely hates'. He also said that she loved rolling in mud and eating chocolate and wine gums, 'the same as any old lady'. But during filming for the BBC programme, *The One Show*, Andy unwisely said 'Hats off to Bobby' with reference to Anne's good condition and the fact she had lived so long. The remarks attracted the ire of animal rights groups and were later mentioned in the Robertses' court case.

When Anne first arrived at Longleat, Jon described her as an 'absolutely beautiful animal' and a 'special old lady': 'When I first saw her and the vets saw her, she was exceptionally lame in her back legs. We changed her treatments and now we've got her here. She's gambolling around and playing in the sand, rubbing and using the scratching posts, almost like her own little spa.' He compared the regular sand baths she gave herself to exfoliating scrubs. But the one thing they didn't know about was Anne's personality, routine and training. And for that, they needed Bobby. Despite many seeing it as controversial to invite him down, Jon says it was crucial for getting to know her. 'Bobby was instrumental in the first few days because he taught my team how he managed things and what commands he used and what she was capable of. Now obviously we weren't doing things like tub stands or anything like that, it was just the basic movements. She still obeys them but it's different now. So she responds a lot and she responds well.'

Jon says that Bobby came to Longleat to teach the team what she liked, what food she ate and what she didn't eat, and adds: 'Without Bobby we'd probably have been slower in our learning curve. He really accelerated it so he was integral in those first few days in allowing us to get on and look after Anne.' Longleat's then chief executive David Bradley insisted she was getting 'younger by the day' and added: 'We've been joking that she may last longer than some of us.' He has also since left the park.

A few weeks after Anne came to Longleat, BBC1's *The One Show* took Moira and Bobby Roberts down to see her. The programme started filming in Anne's barn, where Moira told the reporter: 'If you look in her eyes she's not unhappy. I don't care what anyone says. To us she's never been an animal. She means as much to us as our children do.' The programme then took the couple down to Longleat to Anne's enclosure, where they were filmed stroking her as she played about in the background. In one farcical scene, as Moira told the reporter how much she missed Anne, Anne scooped up some sand with her trunk and threw it in Moira's face. It proved that the elephant had learned a few things about comic timing during her life at the circus. The reporter started laughing while Moira branded Anne a 'troublesome teenager'. When asked whether they should have given Anne up to a retirement home earlier, Moira replied: 'There's nothing the matter with the circus life. I loved the circus life and I like to think Anne loved it as much as we do.'

It was to be the last time the couple visited Anne. Jon says that the then-management at Longleat did not want an ongoing relationship with the Robertses but the couple also say that they could not afford to come down. He says that instead, Bobby and Moira phoned regularly to check on her for the first eighteen months she was at Longleat.

Once she was settled in, it was time to get to know her and for her keepers to forge lasting bonds with her. They were initially struck by her intelligence and her rationality. They told me that when she first arrived, she spotted a sapling poking out near a fence that she liked the look of. As it had previously just been the rhinos living there and they hadn't been able to reach over the fence, it remained untouched – and appetising. So Anne devised a plan. Her former keeper Ryan says: 'There was this one sapling just growing on the bank so she walked over to the fence and reached over but she couldn't quite reach it so immediately she looked round and there was a log several feet behind her. So she went over and got the log, rolled the log over to the fence and then stood on that and that just gave her the extra stretch. It was a real problem solving movement.' Ryan was deeply impressed by her initiative: 'We have several members of staff working here who wouldn't have worked that out. That was a stand-out moment for me.' Andy Hayton said at the time that she had a 'huge personality' but added: 'She can also be awkward, like a four-tonne mother-in-law, but you just look at her and think: "God, the things you've seen, the memories you must have."' She also proved a popular attraction. By Christmas, she had so much fanmail that staff at Longleat had to create a wall for her where they pinned up the scores of cards and letters sent by her admirers.

Dr Ros Clubb from the RSPCA recalls her settling in. 'When I went up to see her the first time she had this big scratching post, big tree trunks,' she says. 'It's really important for elephants to be able to look after their own skin and she was having such a good old scratch and it was lovely to see. I think it can be quite irritating for them [without posts] because it just builds up into layers all over their body.' She adds: 'I remember that she had a big mound of sand in her enclosure and she instantly went for it and started frolicking like a little calf. It was amazing and she's this old arthritic lady and she was just in her element. She was rolling in it and throwing it on herself; it was just lovely. She was scratching like crazy on every bit she could get to with the scratching post. She was a completely different elephant by then as she had been on the pain medication. There was one tree trunk that was horizontal to the floor and she was rubbing the underneath of her belly on it and she was in all sorts of positions to get to the nooks and crannies. It was great.'

Though the RSPCA weren't thrilled with Anne's first home at Longleat, they believed it was the best possible outcome. 'It wasn't ideal but it's better than what she had,' says Ros. 'Jon will admit himself it was an old elephant house and she was time-sharing it with a rhino at that point so she only had half of the enclosure. So it wasn't ideal by any stretch of the imagination, but the fact that she was on the right drugs, she had access to the sand and the scratching posts, she was getting brows [tree branches] and getting looked after and treated like an elephant – I think that as an emergency treatment that was great. Our next step was how can we make this better, because it's not a long-term solution and we had a lot of discussions with Longleat about how they could make things better in the current circumstances.'

Her colleague Jody Gordon, an inspector at the RSPCA's Special Operations Unit, said that her transformation had proven how unhealthy she was when she was at the circus. 'She was a different animal. Her body shape changed in the space of a few months because of her muscle growth and you could see it in her behaviour,' he says. 'She was such an old, captive elephant that I don't think even at the time we expected her to still be alive now despite the fact we obviously wanted to do everything we could for her.'

Although Anne stole the limelight as Britain's largest

celebrity, she wasn't the only animal to be liberated from the Robertses' circus: Monty the camel was also set free. In one of the more shocking scenes of callous and unprovoked behaviour on the video, Nitu can be seen to spit in Monty's face. He also beat, kicked and jabbed him with a pitchfork. The seven-year-old, who was born in captivity, was released to freedom and introduced to other camels for the first time in his life. John Minion, of the Yorkshire Wildlife Park in Doncaster, where he was rehomed, said at the time: 'He's settling in brilliantly. He was a bit shocked by all the space and other animals at first, but he's feeding well and is going to be a big hit.'

Monty, who was originally a present for Bobby's granddaughter Summer, spent most of his life travelling around the country with Anne. He appeared in the ring with horses, clowns, and also Anne before she retired. The RSPCA said at the time: 'There is strong evidence to show that wild animals such as camels are likely to suffer in a travelling circus environment. In addition, camels are a social species and Monty didn't have the company of other camels. The move means that there are no wild animals left at Bobby Roberts [Super] Circus.' Ros Clubb adds: 'It was a big thing to rehome Monty because that meant Bobby went wild-animal free and that was one last circus without animals.'

Sadly, Monty has since died of old age.

Although Anne's home at Longleat was only ever supposed to be temporary, Jon had the idea that they could turn it into an elephant sanctuary, something which was badly needed in Europe to rehome all the elephants from circuses and safari parks that were no longer wanted. He said at the time: 'When we move forward this area will be a sanctuary for elephants, part of which, a very small amount of it, will be on show but a lot of it will be off show as well so we can give real respect and dignity to the animals as they live out their lives.' Justifying the need for a sanctuary, he said: 'There are still quite a lot of African elephants around but Asian elephants are limited to about 28,000 in the world and 16,000 of them are actually in camps in captivity so there is a reality where Asian elephants could be at a point where they're extinct in my lifetime, which is phenomenally depressing. So there's a huge vested interest in these animals and people will support the concept if they feel it's being done with the highest welfare standards, which is definitely what we're going to do.'

The *Daily Mail* pledged its support and launched a funding campaign in April 2011 to encourage its readers to donate. Celebrity supporters jumped on board. *X Factor* judge Simon Cowell was one of the first to make a significant donation. He said: 'I have followed this story for the last few days. Thank you to the *Mail* for highlighting this appalling cruelty and I hope this will help all the similar animals also in distress. I urge everyone to get behind this campaign.' Amanda Holden, of *Britain's Got Talent*, was equally supportive: 'It greatly saddened me to hear of the plight of Anne the elephant. These beautiful creatures deserve our respect, and I am glad she now has the care she deserves.' A spokesman for Princess Michael of Kent said: 'She is 100 per cent behind this and thinks that it is a really important story.' Even the fascinating Lord Bath, who owns the Wiltshire reserve and is said to keep a harem of 'wifelets', said: 'We are delighted that Anne has arrived at Longleat and seems to have settled in so quickly.' Naturalist and TV star Bill Oddie was yet another prominent supporter of the campaign: 'I was delighted when I read of Anne's release from captivity. I am completely against performing animals in circuses and I think it should be illegal. Even if they are not abused or injured, I believe that animals are not there for our amusement or entertainment. They should be treated with dignity.' TV gardener Alan Titchmarsh, entertainer Uri Geller and author Jilly Cooper also pledged their support for Anne's new home.

It was later decided that Anne wouldn't be rehomed with other elephants. And though there can be no doubt that Jon was right about the need for a sanctuary, unfortunately, following further consultation, it was agreed that Longleat wasn't the right place for it. But what was most important was that she had found happiness and a home. Chris Draper of the Born Free Foundation remembers seeing her just after she moved in and being amazed by the transformation. 'I do recall seeing some footage quite early on of her just being an elephant, which was incredible. I'd not seen her do anything other than stand there and sway and look a bit vacant prior to that. To watch her going to town with a tyre on a chain – not the most imaginative of enrichments, but she seemed to be having a whale of a time with it – and rolling around in that sand pile that they'd put in, that was quite gratifying and definitely an improvement on what she'd had previously.'

Anne's keeper Ross Ellis adds: 'Watching her go from how she was then to now is amazing. It's a massive reward for me. We've worked so hard to get her in a good condition. She's happy now.'

CHAPTER 5

ANNE'S BEGINNINGS IN THE JUNGLE

Born in Sri Lanka at some point in the early 1950s, Anne was taken from her mother and her home and shipped in a crate to Britain. There is considerable disagreement about the exact circumstances of her life before being bought by Bobby Roberts' father.

In Bobby's version, she was born to a captive mother who lived with a mahout. 'I was just a little boy,' he recalls. 'There used to be a pet shop and [the owner] had a shed at the bottom of the garden with a sack over it and he'd have two or three elephants over there. You'd go there and say that one and that one.' She was sold to his father for £3,000 – around £90,000 in today's money.

According to ADI and the Born Free Foundation, Anne was taken from a wild herd and kidnapped from the jungle and her mother by poachers at the age of about four. This is based on the idea that there were no captive breeding programmes in Sri Lanka at the time. There are no written records that could be traced to determine the truth. What little is known is based on an entry on an online database – elephant.se – which has since been taken down. It would clearly not have existed at the time she was born so it is difficult to know how much to rely on it. She was imported during the time of a huge influx of elephants destined for European circuses before the Convention on International Trade in Endangered Species of Wild Fauna and Flora was made law in 1975.

Because there are no records, there is disagreement about how exactly she would have been removed from her mother and the possibilities range from the prosaic to the distressing. ADI described one harrowing method: Poachers would stalk a herd of elephants in the jungle and then slaughter all the adult females before trapping the calves as they tried to comfort their dying mothers.

Bobby Roberts says that the dealer they bought her from said she was born to a captive mother who lived with a mahout, but says that as his father bought him he cannot be sure. Chris Draper of the Born Free Foundation also believes she would have been born in the wild as he thinks that there were no captive breeding programmes in Sri Lanka in the 1950s, something Jon Cracknell agrees with. But Asian elephant expert Khyne U Mar thinks that Anne's good behaviour and longevity indicate that she was born to a captive mother. The truth is not known.

Although almost unheard of now, circuses with wild animals were big business in the 1950s and it was then normal for exotic and endangered creatures to be snatched from their habitats and brought to Europe. Tigers, elephants and lions were part of almost every big circus. Harrods in London once sold elephants, panthers and tigers and had a collection of animals that was said to rival London Zoo. And it wasn't just circuses buying them. Future American president Ronald Reagan, then the governor of California, rang up Harrods to buy a baby elephant called Gertie in 1967. Legend has it the shop worker on the other end of the phone said: 'Would that be African or Indian, sir?' Playwright Noël Coward was also a famous customer, having had an alligator bought for him for Christmas in 1951. The section, which first opened its doors in 1917, finally closed in 2014 to make way for a womenswear section.

The public still loves the magic of circuses, but today the company Cirque du Soleil, featuring acrobats and street performance by humans without performing animals, is the kind they prefer. Gone are the days in which lions jumped through flaming hoops and elephants stood on tubs. The word 'circus' comes from the Latin for circle and was used by the Romans to describe their venues for gladiator battles and feeding live Christians to lions. But the circus as we know it was invented in England in 1768 by a horse trainer named Philip Astley, according to the website Circopedia, which gives a history. Astley introduced jugglers, clowns and acrobats to fill the gaps in between his equestrian performances. He is also credited with having discovered the perfect diameter for a circus ring – enough space to get a horse up to a gallop and still be able to balance on its back – and this is now the international standard for all circus rings.

Back then, circuses were popular entertainment and almost all featured animals. Christmas television slots were dominated by live circus performance and became a British tradition. But as animal rights groups started to make an impression in the 1980s, performing animals fell out of favour. Local councils increasingly banned them from cities. Circuses began to focus on the once peripheral acts of tightrope walkers and sword swallowers. Now, while there are still around fifty circuses in Britain today, only a handful of these present domestic animals like horses and dogs. And only three present exotic animals. In Britain today, there are lions, tigers, snakes, a camel, a raccoon and an Ankole – an African bull with enormous horns.

Anne originated from a different era when elephants were bought for circuses and she was once one of a herd of twelve who performed with the Robertses' family. Though there are no records of her birth, her capture or training, she would almost certainly have had a similar start to other elephants taken from their natural habitats and their mothers at that time.

Those who claim to know the most about Anne's history, apart from Bobby Roberts himself, are Jan Creamer and Tim Phillips, ADI's founders. ADI had been monitoring her situation since 1995, when concerns first started to be raised about her welfare, and researched her history. Tim says that Anne came to Britain at a time when circuses were as popular a form of entertainment as cinemas are now. 'Anne would have arrived in the heyday of circuses in the 1960s when there were massive sell-out shows and great herds of elephants who were all destined to die young,' he says. 'There were lions, tigers, bears and everything. It was the era of the Chipperfield Circus on television. The 1950s and 60s were the glory days of the circus industry. In the 1970s, it was still holding its own but it started to decline from then on. In the 1980s, it was starting to come under pressure from animal rights groups but it was still very strong in the 1990s. In 1996, there were sixteen elephants touring the UK. This is a very small country to have sixteen elephants touring it and, obviously, Anne was one of those.'

So ADI began the undercover investigations. What they discovered when they rigged up a secret camera in the barn was that her traumatic life was even worse than they had imagined. It revealed that she was subjected to severe physical suffering but it also left her with lasting psychological damage that is observed all too often in captive animals.

For Anne, that psychological damage would have started young. Before ever reaching the UK, she may have been 'broken', a horrific process that involved crushing her spirit and will through punishment and starvation before she could be trained. Usually it is a process carried out by a mahout, originally a word from the Indian language Sanskrit meaning 'elephant keeper'.

ADI boss Jan Creamer has carried out investigations of this practice and describes how it works for elephants taken from the wild. 'There are no records of Anne's particular early training but the traditional training methods are still the same today,' she says. 'They put the baby elephant into a crush box, which is basically a really small box, and tie its legs up. They crush its body so it can't move around. It goes through a period of that whilst being beaten. It will then be confined to the box for days and days until its spirit is broken.'

According to Jan, the creature is also beaten with bullhooks until it can't fight back anymore. She goes on: 'What they need is for the animal to just give up psychologically so any sense of self-preservation, any sense of independence, any will, is crushed and broken. That's how they do it. So it's days and days in these boxes, together with beatings and stretching it out, pulling its legs about, pulling the legs through – just anything deeply unpleasant to make it give in.'

Anne may have suffered more than other elephants due to her large size, believes Jan. 'The chances are that because Anne is a large elephant, she would have taken longer to break in than others,' she explains. 'It would have taken weeks and months. Mahouts work in teams. There would have been one main mahout who would have been her main trainer and contact and then they'll also have had a group of others who assist because obviously it can take several people.'

'It's really violent,' says Tim. 'If she left Sri Lanka at that age then she would have been broken when she arrived [in Britain]. She was wild-caught, we know that, so she was torn from her mother and her natural habitat and almost certainly broken to get her compliant. She's a big animal so they take some beating so that they think: "I am going to obey everything" when the mahout has a bullhook or a stick leaning by their side. That's a serious level of intimidation.'

Dr Khyne U Mar, who has featured on many BBC documentaries about elephants and is known as the 'Elephant Lady of Burma' (now Myanmar), has expanded on the concept based on her first-hand experience. The practices of Burma, she says, are the same across Asia. 'If you have wild-caught calves, you have to break them immediately after capture. When the elephant's spirit is broken they follow commands and do what the human wants them to do. They are put in a crush box and their mobility is restricted and their food is restricted so they're hungry. Then they get food as a reward when they start training.' She says that violence was often part of the breaking, though it didn't have to be. 'The process is usually done with food or fear,' she adds. 'If the elephant does not do what it's told, the keepers start beating it and punishing it. This is when the abusive behaviour starts setting in.' She says that the length of the process depends on the elephant's personality, but they usually needed to be in the crush box for a few weeks; it is normal for a female to take two weeks, but males can be resistant and so the training can take longer. Once it is successfully broken, the elephant is prepared for a life of servitude to humans.

This is not how any of us think of mahouts when we journey to Asia and see them with their elephants. We think of it as a tradition steeped in history and we regard the relationship between a mahout and his elephant as mutually respectful. Mahouts work, eat and sleep with their elephant and appear to have a special bond with it. But as elephants are wild, dangerous creatures who do not choose to mix with humans it leaves many wondering at what price their obedience is obtained. The equipment used by mahouts suggests that it is not an equal relationship but one where one party dominates another. The bullhook – or ankus or goad –

which is essentially a metal hook at the end of a pole, is used as an instrument of control. It is used to guide the elephant and is applied on the creature's pressure points, in the head, mouth and inner ear, where it is most sensitive.

Because of this, many believe that the bullhook causes the elephant pain and debate rages about the ethics behind its use. Two American cities – Los Angeles and Oakland, both in California – have banned its use, but advocates say it is a necessary instrument of control and does not hurt the elephant. They argue that it is merely a useful method of elongating the arm and enabling the mahout to interact with the elephant. Its defenders also insist that bullhooks are a necessity in parts of the world practising what is known as 'free contact' as there is no other way to control the elephant. This is essentially the concept of controlling the elephant by interacting with it physically as opposed to protected contact, which is when the captive animal is free to move around as it pleases and has no direct contact with humans.

This is likely to be the sort of background that Anne came from. Torn from her mother and her home after being broken, she arrived in Britain to begin her new life. It was a sad start for an elephant destined to spend the majority of her days in a circus.

CHAPTER 6

LIFE AT THE CIRCUS

In one now infamous photo, Anne sits on a tub, rearing unnaturally on her hind legs as her owner grins for the camera. In the background is his brightly-coloured van emblazoned with the words 'Bobby Roberts Super Circus'. It's a haunting and dated image, a relic from a past era in a world where circuses were primetime entertainment and performing animals their biggest stars. The jolly photo conceals the cruel reality of what animals like Anne, Britain's last circus elephant, had to endure to become the Big Top's main attraction. It reveals nothing of the life of performance and exploitation she and other creatures suffered after being snatched from their natural habitats and put to work in the circus.

Anne was once a big circus star and a popular attraction. She and her fellow elephants paraded down the street from the train station to the showground to announce the arrival of the circus in town. Her photo was pasted up on billboards and children queued to have their picture taken with her. But times changed and attitudes followed them. Circuses increasingly abandoned exotic animal acts as discomfort grew over their lives and conditions until Anne was the last circus elephant left in Britain.

Suddenly, instead of the star performer she was a throwback, a symbol of a bygone age when circuses dominated the television schedules and elephants competed with brightly painted clowns and daring trapeze artists for the spotlight. As her movements became more faltering – a legacy of her age and arthritis – the disquiet over her life of servitude and drudgery grew. In around 2006, she was retired from appearing in the main shows, but was still rolled out to pose for pictures for £6 a time during the interval.

As the Robertses' circus travelled the country, playing to increasingly dwindling audiences, a growing chorus of animal rights protesters followed it and dogged its every move. The moment the circus pitched up in a town, complaints were filed with the local council. These were often successful and Bobby was refused permission for Anne to perform and on one occasion, for photos to be taken of her. It didn't seem to be an ideal life for our largest land mammal more commonly used to patrolling large areas of forest and jungle in the company of its family. But what was life really like for her in the greatest show on earth?

Every circus season she was forced to perform painful and demeaning tricks such as having to rear up on her hind legs – something vets say causes incredible pressure on the back hips. As mentioned earlier, she drags at least one of her back legs due to arthritis now. She also had to stand on a tiny stool and gallop around the ring with various performers on her back, like dancers and clowns. Furthermore, when the circus closed after the summer season every year, she stayed in crowded winter quarters, shackled by iron chains round her ankles which allowed her to move just a step or so to each side.

When she was touring, the journeys were long and often not broken up, according to ADI, who say they monitored her movements for years. Tim claims that she regularly did eighteen-hour trips in a transporter in which she and the other animals were chained so that they couldn't move around. ADI claim they saw elephants whipped during a circus performance in 1995, and that they had to live in a car park when the circus visited Glasgow in 2000. After that, they claim that they followed the elephant truck from Glasgow back down to Polebrook and saw the circus stop for the night on the way without taking the elephants out. On another expedition on 16 June 2002 from Blackpool to

Carlisle, they claim that Anne spent nineteen hours in a transporter. Bobby and Moira deny these allegations.

And it wasn't just the performance aspect that would have impacted on her. The realities of travelling circuses are harsh ones for animals. Constantly having to move from place to place, they endure being transported in beastwagons for long stretches of time. They have to be restrained within these trailers and then they must wait to be offloaded. The circuses then set up on whatever land is available, which is often insufficient for their needs given that in the wild they would normally have vast tracts of land to roam. For health and safety reasons, they are usually confined to secure areas in small areas of space, surrounded by electric fence or chained to wooden pallets. Bobby Roberts says he used to take the elephants out at service stations and walk them on the grass verges but that is simply unimaginable nowadays.

During the 1990s, about the time ADI started monitoring Anne, she was touring with the Robertses' circus with two other elephants, Beverly and Janie. ADI's Tim Phillips says she would have spent her summer performing and being transported up and down the country in a 47ft trailer before spending the winter locked up in a barn. He says: 'When an animal travels with the circus, it gets put in there before anything is packed up. It may take the whole evening to pack everything up, which means the animal's stuck in the transporter overnight.' He explains that the circus would set off in the early hours, so Anne, Beverly and Janie would be in the transporter together and they'd all be chained up in crowded and hot conditions. Then they'd be moved to the circus site.

'They'd probably stay in there until they put the whole circus up, with the Big Top and the rest of it,' adds Tim. 'Then, if the workers are tired, they may still leave the elephants in there, so they would be pretty disgusting and stinky conditions by then.' For the next week or two weeks that the circus spent at the site, the animals would live in a small pen, probably not much bigger than ten by ten metres and surrounded by electric tape, he says, adding that they would be chained in there for most of the time.

Tim claims that Bobby used to chain the elephants up and cover the chains with hay. 'There are photos of that,' he says. 'They'd be standing there, looking like they were free, and people would think: "Blimey, they haven't moved at all during the show." But people glance and they don't notice.' Even if they got some time to wander around in their pens, they would still be chained for most of the time; they'd be chained before and after the performances before being taken to bed after the final one. 'Then they'll be on the chains all night and if they're lucky, they'll be let off in the morning.' They might be allowed loose as early as 8am, but more likely 10am. 'So they get a window of about five hours where they're not immobilised – a very, very small period,' he concludes.

Referring specifically to Anne, he says that most of the time she was chained on the front leg and opposite back leg. 'Bobby would switch the chains over. He wouldn't even let her walk about,' he says. 'He'd just switch from one leg to the other on her front leg and then the alternate back leg. And those chains are stretched out to a pin, which is underneath the board they're standing on. They can't tug them out, they can't move. They're not stretched out, but it means they can move pretty much one step to the side, one step back, and that's where a lot of that stereotypic behaviour kicks in, like the rocking you see, because the animal is really, really frustrated and going out of its mind with boredom and it's also trying to alleviate the pressure.'

Tim says that the three elephants – Anne, Beverly and Janie – always lived together and went into the ring trunk to tail. 'They would do pirouettes, hind leg stands, all the traditional things. They used to be ridden by three women in the ring. Bobby would present it,' he says.

Jan Creamer adds: 'They were forced to do tricks standing on the tub, which looks a bit like a drum. They would do hind leg stands. All of those things which vets now say if you have them standing on their hind legs like that all the time you're putting incredible pressure on their hip joints and their legs. The other challenge you've got here in the UK for elephants is that they're not designed to live in this climate. It's damp and cold and they're suited to the hot and dry with occasional wet but it dries quickly. It has an effect on their joints.'

Meanwhile, trouble was brewing. In 2001, after a decade or so of touring with each other, Anne's companions Beverly and Janie died suddenly. Bobby says that Beverly was poisoned. Moira Roberts told me: 'This little boy came to Bobby and said: "A man's just fed that elephant with poison in an apple." Bobby said: "Don't be silly." She was dead the next morning.' She says that they had a post-mortem investigation conducted by specialist vet Andrew Greenwood, but it was inconclusive. Janie died of a mixture of old age and pining away, she adds, and the Robertses say they had both elephant bodies cremated. However, ADI were unsatisfied with the explanation as there was no official report. Jan says: 'We couldn't find any reports apart from one from him saying they had died and that was it and no one seemed to investigate. I would have thought that someone should have investigated.' It meant that by the 2000s, Anne was alone on the road, as the Robertses' remaining elephant.

Circuses were already coming under real pressure. In 1998, ADI carried out a big undercover operation that exposed Mary Chipperfield. Tim reflects: 'Mary Chipperfield Promotions was the factory for lions and tigers. They supplied over 1,000 tigers for acts across Europe. Then that was gone and, one by one, all the circuses were going and these sixteen elephants that were touring the UK slowly disappeared. Circus King closed down and they had three elephants. Circus Hoffman went and they had six. Mary Chipperfield regularly had five out on the road with different circuses and they all went; most of them went to zoos, some went to overseas. So it was suddenly quite a small industry and it was trying to make itself look better.'

Tim says this change meant all circus owners were more conscious of their image and their animals' welfare. 'So now Anne would get the pretty pathetic-looking paddock outdoors during the showtime so she'd be on grass but visitors could see her in there. Then they'd stick her on chains ready for the show and it was pretty much the same routine. These enclosures are pathetic – it's just a bit of grass,' he says.

In 2010, ADI again followed Anne on tour, describing her as 'this ageing exhibit'. By that point, she was travelling with seven Arabian stallions, six Falabella horses and two dogs, which all featured in the circus's 110-minute performance. Although she was only rolled out for photo calls, they say she still suffered as she needed to be controlled. 'It is a performance requiring a high level of control just to plod these elephants around children and have them come out on command and do their little circuit,' Tim explains. 'For some, that's the entire act, like for instance at Jolly's Circus, where a fox sits on a horse and goes round and round the ring. So she would still consider herself to be performing and having this terrible life.'

At about this time, ADI took more footage of Anne in an outdoor area, with three workers trying to get her back to her barn. She is shown ambling along before pausing, engaged by a branch. The workers try to push her so she keeps walking, but she is much more interested in the branch and ignores them. So they get out a pair of pliers and grab her ear with them. At first, she resists, unwilling to move, and still far more interested in the branch – but then they tug harder and, clearly in pain, she has no choice but to walk on. It is only reasonable to assume that the workers had used the pliers on her before, otherwise, why would they have them with them? It's a sad reminder of the suffering she endured before being set free.

ADI weren't the only ones monitoring her. Chris Draper, of the Born Free Foundation, says he too spent time following the circus around and noting her condition. He remembers seeing Anne and worrying about her arthritis. 'I'd seen her several times on the road and I'd always been very concerned about her gait in particular. I remember years and years ago watching her really slowly clambering down a grassy bank in order to do a photo shoot with Bobby Roberts while I was sitting in a car park outside the circus. I remember thinking just how sort of torturous that was for her to do that given what was already a problem with her gait and her legs, which looked very much like arthritis at the time.' He says this would have been around 2005–7 and though she managed to 'lumber' down the bank, she clearly wasn't on good form.

Chris says despite her care, her gait hadn't significantly changed as it was likely that the damage done to her body from performing was permanent. 'It hasn't changed much, it's still the same, the dragging of the feet,' he says. 'But that implies to me that she's not a mobile animal and needed proper care for her arthritis rather than to be loaded into a van each week and shipped off here, there and everywhere.'

Chris also believes that Bobby used some kind of implement on Anne to ensure she behaved – something Bobby vehemently denies. Chris recalls a time in 2008 when he says he saw Bobby use it on her while she was posing for photographs. 'During a performance, Anne was led into the ring in the interval. She got to stand there while he stood next to her, while kids came up and positioned themselves next to her on the other side and a photo was taken. It was like a conveyor belt of kids having their photo taken on Polaroid for a pound a pop. Anne was vaguely interested in some tufts of grass that were sprouting through some sawdust in the ring and was just idly picking at them with her trunk. Bobby didn't like that. I remember him yanking her trunk away a few times and she sort of stood there, looking a bit dejected. Then she'd go back to it either absentmindedly or like, "stuff it, it's worth it". He got increasingly angry, smacking her, shouting at her and pulling her ear. Then she obviously did it one time too many and all I can say is that I witnessed his hand go into his jacket pocket on his chest, pull out some item – I don't know what it was – and basically jab it very quickly behind her ear, to which she recoiled. That's all I saw. I suspect it was something sharp and he jabbed it behind her ear because she was misbehaving in his view.' Chris believes he also saw Bobby use the sharp instrument when leading Anne into the truck to be taken away to Longleat, though Jon says he didn't see it. Again, Bobby strongly denies this.

Chris adds that although he was pleased that her suffering came to light, it shouldn't have to take a shocking video to rescue an animal from a bad life. 'Although it's great that the footage of the abuse came to light, and it's appalling and absolutely disgraceful that she was subjected to that, I'm almost disappointed that it has to rely on an animal getting the crap beaten out of it for something to be done,' he says. 'The issue as I see it is how she was being kept and how she was living her life day to day, week to week, year to year. That was the primary issue and it's sad that groups have to do undercover footage and have to prove abuse before anything's done.'

However, not everyone agrees that her life was all bad: Anne's osteopath, Tony Nevin, who has treated some 200 elephants both in Britain and abroad in the last twenty-odd years, has an interesting insight into her life at the circus. He treated her in 2007 when she had retired but was still touring with the Robertses. Her arthritis had attracted a lot of ire from animal rights activists who had started protesting at the circus while it was at Cheltenham Racecourse, near his practice. One of Tony's customers gave Bobby Roberts his number. 'Bobby rang me up and said: "We've got an elephant and people have been saying that she's elderly and shouldn't be travelling and that. Could you come and have a look at her?"' Tony recalls. But unlike the animal rights campaigners who say she suffered a miserable life on tour with the circus, Tony actually thinks Anne was doing rather well. He describes her circus accommodation as the 'lap of luxury' – 'She didn't sleep in the trailer. She had a whopping great marquee and a giant straw bed made up for her. It was like going in to some Bedouin camp when I saw her.' After doing a consultation with vets, he found it was all 'above board' and 'she was great': 'She was suffering all the symptoms of older age, wear and tear and osteoarthritis, and so we did some work with her. Apart from having arthritis she was in very good shape, she was fit. Mentally, she was much more content than most zoo elephants. It was only later on that she started stereotyping, she certainly wasn't stereotyping when I first met her. I probably put that down to the fact that she had such a varied lifestyle so she got to swim in the sea, she got to go on beaches, go across moorland... All sorts of stuff she's done over the years. Then you look at most zoo ones and they're plodding around the same paddock.'

CHAPTER 7

BOBBY THEN – PART ONE

There are elephants stitched on the cushions in the cosy trailer Bobby and Moira Roberts call home. There are elephant pictures on the walls, china elephant statues on the shelves and elephant magnets on the fridge. In the kitchen, a framed tapestry of an elephant looking sad says: 'I'll never forget.'

There can be no doubt that the couple loved the animals that for more than half a decade were their constant companions on the vast farm they own in the genteel village of Polebrook in Northamptonshire. 'Bobby lived and breathed elephants,' Moira says simply. 'And they loved him.'

Against the odds, given the circumstances under which I'd met them, they granted me an interview.

Though wary, they shared with me their memories of life in the golden days of the Great British Circus. They travelled the world meeting royalty, top brass and the cream of the celebrity world, with their troupe of six elephants in tow. At one point, they had fifteen elephants. They were known to everyone they met as Bobby, Moira and 'the girls'.

Anne, the couple's ever-present companion throughout their circus lives, was fed by Her Majesty The Queen, performed for the then Indian Prime Minister Rajiv Gandhi and once met English comedian Freddie Starr. She swam in the sea at Blackpool, went up the Eiffel Tower and appeared on television. Whatever your opinions on the ethics of elephants in circuses, it's hard not to be fascinated by the Robertses' lives. Their memories are of elephants travelling by train and parading through the streets to the circus, cheered on by the townsfolk. They remember circus performances dominating the Christmas television schedules. Bobby was once a celebrity known as 'the elephant man'. It was a different age.

And no one knows more about it than him. Born into the industry, Bobby Roberts is the seventh generation of his family to work in the circus and can trace his lineage back hundreds of years to Nelson's time. His children and their children have followed him into the business and his grandchildren are the tenth generation to work in the circus.

Anne was bought by Bobby's father, Bobby Roberts

senior, and was later inherited by his son. At that time, elephants were part of all big circuses. And the Robertses began their career with the very biggest and best. They were members of the famous dynasty of Sir Robert Fossett, one of the originators of the circus. Bobby, now seventy-two, founded his own Bobby Roberts Super Circus in 1993 but cut his teeth at his late father and uncle's circus.

Their history is fascinating. For nearly forty years, as the Robertses tell me, Bobby senior and his brother Tommy ran one of the most popular travelling circuses in Britain. Bobby recalls when his father and uncle started the circus just after the war and didn't have any proper transporting equipment. 'I remember at the old farm where we used to live they had a little old bus and they used to stick the poles through the windows because they didn't have a lorry. They always put on a good show.' Bobby senior enjoyed a distinguished career in the industry and for many years served as honorary president of the Association of Circus Proprietors of Great Britain.

Bobby senior's father – and Bobby junior's grandfather – was Paul Otto, an acrobat who came to Britain in the early twentieth century and married Mary Fossett, the sister of Sir Robert Fossett. Born Robert Otto Fossett in 1912, in Kingsthorpe, Northamptonshire, he later took the surname Roberts, as did his brother Tommy. Having started his career as a clown at the age of eleven, he moved on to a solo bareback riding act and later worked as an acrobat alongside his brother, not just in the circus but also in theatres. Through his life on stage, he met Kitty Mednick, a member of a performing family musical act. Robert and Kitty married in 1941, and the following year Bobby junior, their first son, was born.

The brothers soon moved on from performing to running their own travelling circuses and started to lay the foundations for what would later define them: animal training. They renamed their circus the Robert Bros' Hip Hip Zoo Ray Mammoth Circus and acquired their first elephant from Dudley Zoo in 1946. The circus attracted huge audiences and became so successful that it was soon producing animal acts for other shows and circuses, as well as major events, and employed large numbers of animal trainers, clowns and other acts. Bobby senior specialised in training elephants, horses, ponies, dogs and llamas and passed his husbandry skills on to his son. By the early 1950s, the brothers had a full circus and stage show, another summer circus in London and one on the Isle of Man.

At this point, Bobby junior entered the limelight He first presented the elephants in 1961 and later appeared with them several times before the Queen and the Royal Family. By the early 1970s, the circus had a dozen or more elephants as well as horses, ponies and exotic animals and Bobby had taken over the animal showing.

As the big circuses Billy Smart and Bertram Mills disappeared, the Robertses' circus became one of the biggest on the road and later secured a lucrative contract to show its performances on the BBC. The family soon became household names and their performances were shown around the world. An episode of *Songs of Praise* was filmed at their circus in around 2000. Meanwhile, as the brothers' families grew, they decided to split and Bobby formed the Roberts Brothers Super Circus with his sons. In 1993, Bobby began his own circus, Bobby Roberts Super Circus, after splitting with his younger brother Tommy, who went on to show horses and ponies at Zippo's Circus.

The death of Bobby Roberts senior, one of the great circus proprietors, heralded the end of the golden age of the Great British travelling circus, which had first been created in Britain in 1768. Nevertheless, Bobby junior continued with his father's legacy. Like almost all circus people, he had started as a clown, making his stage debut at the age of four. As a child and young man, he had learned acrobatics, bareback riding and wire walking but his proudest achievement of all was his work with elephants. Bobby says he was a leading elephant husbandry expert and zoos, circuses and handlers from all over the world sought him out for his knowledge and experience. He also toured all over Europe with his elephants, telling the BBC: 'I've always worked with animals, but since I was about four years old I've come in with my dad and trained the horses and trained everything you can think of. Elephants were my thing.' Until 2011, and the fallout from Anne's story, he had a good reputation in circus circles for animal husbandry and his performances still drew large, if gradually dwindling, crowds around the country. Bureaucracy took its toll on the business too and Bobby referred to it as a 'dream for health and safety officers'.

Asked about his favourite memories of Anne and the other elephants, he says it was the 'simple things'. 'They all had individual traits,' he recalls. 'Bev [Beverly] used to tap on the floor with her trunk, Anne used to talk to you, another used to screech through her tongue like them big fish – you know, killer whales.'

And the elephants had a varied life, to say the least. He would take them to swim in the sea at Blackpool before the crowds arrived. 'When I took them on the beach one would like to go in, one would like to roll in the sand. Some of them didn't want to go in if I didn't go in, or they wanted me with them,' he explains, adding that Anne enjoyed swimming. He shows me pictures of her in the sea with the other elephants. 'I used to go and sit on the steps and the elephants used to go down on the beach. They'd either swim or roll. Janie used to run along and kick all the sandcastles over from the day before and I used to whistle them and they'd all go up the steps and we'd come back.'

But, as with everything about the way of life they

knew, it wasn't to last. A member of the public informed the council of what was happening and Bobby was prevented from taking them there. Moira says: 'She was one of those do-gooder people who think it's cruel in the circus. She managed to stop us going on the beach. They used to get so much pleasure from going down the beach.' His voice tinged with nostalgia, Bobby adds: 'I'd been going there for years. Elephants and horses and everythin'.'

Bobby is happiest speaking about the past; he resists any talk of the present. When I ask him how he feels about losing the circus and the court case, he fidgets uncomfortably. 'A bit sad, like,' he says. 'When you love something so much, you know, it's a difficult thing. The only thing that I do have is I have all the memories and the people that come [to see] me from all over the world. That's all I've got left.'

He gestures at a huge photo frame bursting with pictures of happier times from the circus days. A good proportion of the pictures are of members of the Royal Family meeting the elephants. There is even one with the Queen feeding an elephant. 'The Queen fed Anne a bun that day,' he recalls. 'Then Princess Anne wanted to know where her bun was. That was the following day. We thought we'd get into trouble but Princess Anne said: "Where's my bun?" so I gave her six pieces of sugar and she fed all the elephants sugar.'

In the picture of the Queen, Bobby has his arm around

her back and confesses that he didn't realise he'd broken Royal protocol by doing that. On another occasion he shook her gloveless hand, not realising this was also frowned upon. He is glowing in his praise of the Queen. 'The first time you speak to her she puts you right at ease,' he says. 'Brilliant they are, the whole lot of them.' Moira looks wistful, adding: 'We don't meet Royal Family anymore. We're outcasts.' To which Bobby hilariously replies: 'Yeah, we do. I was at Buckingham Palace the other day with the Water Rats.'

Bobby is a member of the Grand Order of Water Rats, an exclusive fraternity of British performers that includes Queen guitarist Brian May, comedian Ken Dodd and Prince Philip, Duke of Edinburgh, as a companion member. When asked how they reacted to the news of his conviction, he is resolute. 'They were 100 per cent behind me,' he says. Asked if it was difficult for him to face them all, he says: 'No, I was with twenty-odd [Water Rats] yesterday and they all know me so they all know that it was a fallacy.'

Other photographs at Bobby and Moira's home show scores of smiling celebrities in the frame: Bernard Bresslaw from the *Carry On* films, cast members of *Chitty Chitty Bang Bang* and *Hi-de-Hi!*, as well as the magician Paul Daniels and the comedian Jimmy Logan, a close family friend, who the couple named their grandson after.

Bobby tells me Anne met a number of celebrities over the years, including Keith Harris and Orville the duck, as well as the singer and broadcaster Aled Jones. But Moira points out: 'Anne was a celebrity. People came to meet *her*.' The couple also worked with Jimmy Savile a few times and their daughter Kitty was once told to sit on his knee for a photo. They recall her refusing and being very unhappy about the whole situation. 'She must have known,' says Moira.

The Robertses have fond memories of performing in the Berlin Tattoo. Major Michael Parker, a colourful character who organised elaborate state events for the Queen and others, summoned Bobby and the elephants. Moira recalls: 'We got our army numbers, the elephants got their army numbers and we joined the Royal Anglians.' She shows me a trophy they presented her with, which says 'To Bobby, Moira and the girls'. 'The girls were the elephants,' she adds. 'They were always Bobby's girls.'

At one point, she says the Royal Air Force men made a bizarre request to Bobby. 'The RAF men were sick of the Royal Household Cavalry and they said: "Would you mind, Bobby, if we took the camel to the officers' mess" because they used to all bring the little Jack Russells – you know what the cavalry are like. Bobby said: "Help yourself." So the camel went for his dinner in the officers' mess.' Another time, they were again hired by Major Michael Parker, who wanted them to go down the Mall with the cannons behind them, while he rode the lead elephant and a brigadier rode Anne. Moira says: 'Michael Parker looked down on Bobby and said: "They'll be alright, Bob, when the Red Arrows fly overhead, won't they?"' Bobby adds: 'That's how much notice I had. The planes flew over the top of Buckingham Palace. They [the elephants] was alright but I thought: "We've got about thirty-five, forty seconds..." Luckily, they never took no notice.' He adds: 'Them sort of things, I used to take them in my stride in them days because I knew every one of them [the elephants].'

He also recalls how clever the elephants were. During one performance in Brighton, they were given accommodation with electric cables in a box. Bobby refused to allow the elephants in there until they were covered up. Eventually, the staff came up with the idea of knocking nails into the box in the hope that would deter the elephants. But the next day, they returned to find every single nail bent over by the elephants. Bobby says knowingly: 'They didn't touch it but they were just saying: "We know what we're doing."'

The circus coming to town was once heralded by the elephants getting off at the train station and marching to the showground as townsfolk cheered them on. 'You'd get thousands of people lining the streets to watch,' Bobby says. 'Everyone would know the animals would be arriving at the station at 11am and the whole town would turn out to watch and applaud. The elephants were so popular. They'd hold each other's trunks while they marched down the street.' He says on one occasion the elephants arrived at a train station they had been to previously and remembered there being a tap on the wall. One wandered over to the wall and ripped off the pipes with her trunk so they could all drink. 'I didn't get to the tap in time,' explains Bobby. 'She'd pulled it off the wall because there were lead pipes there – yanked it off the wall and was drinking it.' He says that the stationmaster was unimpressed.

Bobby concludes: 'I done some ridiculous things over the years. I never thought about it. People say: "Oh, you can't do that," and I'd do it, you know.' He tells stories of how he had to get an elephant to cross a bridge for a music video for the band The Beautiful South: he cycled across first and she simply followed him. He also convinced an elephant to pick a raffle ticket by using the wet part of its trunk to stick to the paper. Once, on the set of the 1993 film *The Secret Garden*, he even got an elephant to lift a table with its trunk during an earthquake scene. When in Edinburgh for a charity event at a manor house, he was told to bring Anne round the side, but he decided it was too cold and walked her in through the front door. The stories are incredible and often star Anne, who became the couple's last companion.

She was a quiet elephant, they say. 'Anne didn't do anything except look at you,' Moira recalls. 'But she liked to go for a walk, I'll tell you that. She'd be out here in this field with an electric fence, but the clever little sod knew how to get out and Bobby had to go and get her from the woods at the bottom of our fields.' She says Anne liked to roam free on the eleven acres of land that they had at the winter quarters. 'Bobby used to say: "I'll go and get her in a minute because that'll give her a chance to wander about and rub herself against the tree trunks" and then he'd go and bring her home. She never ran away.'

Moira also tells of how, in 2003, Anne decided to wander free on Ayr Racecourse in Scotland while they were touring with the circus. The elephant ran through the streets before finally being returned. 'She decided that she would go and visit someone's garden and people wouldn't understand that she was just away for a walk,' Moira explains. But the people who owned the garden did not understand, 'and we had to sort it out'. She says the headlines came thick and fast about how Anne had run away from the circus but adds: 'We knew how to put up with it then.'

The 9ft-tall elephant used to stand on her hind legs, lie down and pirouette in the circus ring for ten minutes in every show. She apparently liked to search people's pockets for sweets and would travel up and down the country in a 47ft articulated truck.

As Bobby recounts the past, Moira sits beside him protectively, helping when he struggles for words, correcting him when he forgets dates and prompting stories. She is hugely defensive of him and almost acts as his bridge between his past and present, protecting him from the harsh realities of life outside the circus. Those who know the couple say he relies on her utterly. It is Moira who agrees to the interview for this book, while Bobby says he would rather not have participated. She feels she has the right to defend the industry more than most as she wasn't born into it and instead ran away to join the circus.

Brought up in the sleepy market town of Castle Douglas in southern Scotland, Moira went to live with her aunt in Glasgow at the age of fourteen following the death of her parents. Her aunt was in the fairground business, which shared space with the circus that Edinburgh-born Bobby was in. At the age of twenty-three, Moira became an usherette in the circus to bring in a bit of money. Despite being five years his senior – she is now seventy-seven – she caught the then eighteen-year-old Bobby's eye – 'because she was the only fairground person who didn't smoke and didn't drink,' he says – and they became an item.

But their families were less than impressed. Hers hated 'circus people' – when Bobby came round, her uncle would say: 'That jungle boy's here again' – and Bobby's family, the circus dynasty, 'abhorred' anyone who wasn't circus. Bobby's father called her 'that loud-mouth traveller'. Moira says carefully: 'It wasn't easy.' But the star-crossed lovers forged ahead regardless. They celebrated their fifty-year anniversary in 2015. As Moira recalled at the time: 'Bobby's dad's stipulation –

and I gave into him like a fool – was that I should join the circus for a year and if we still felt the same way, we'd get married. So I joined the circus at the beginning of '65 and we got married at the end of '65 and it's fifty years now so I like to think we proved them wrong.' Bobby is also unapologetic: 'We fell in love and we've been ever since,' he says.

For Moira, it was something of a baptism of fire. 'I was a complete novice when I joined the circus,' she admits. Having lived a sheltered early life, the circus was different to anything she'd ever known. Suddenly she was surrounded by exotic and otherworldly creatures: lions, tigers, elephants and even polar bears, which Bobby's father kept and trained. She first met Anne when she went down to the circus winter quarters at Polebrook for Bobby's twenty-first birthday.

Her first job was to care for the baby elephants that would arrive at the circus as four-year-olds. She sat up all night with them and cooked them a kind of sweetened rice pudding. Anne was one of those elephants and the couple recall that she loved having her tongue tickled and would pull them in for a cuddle by gently wrapping her trunk round their legs. 'I was terrified at the beginning,' Moira admits. 'They were only little tiny things. I watched Bobby perform but I'd never been close up to the animals.' But she soldiered on. 'I soon grew to love them just as much as he did,' she says.

As a member of the circus, Moira was also expected

to perform. Luckily, she was already pretty nifty with a bow and arrow from her work at the fairground so Bobby's mother came up with an act for her as an Indian to Bobby's cowboy, with his sharp shooting and horses. Unfortunately, one day the performance ended in disaster. Moira recalls: 'I used to hold a balloon in my mouth and I would blow it up against the target and Bobby would shoot the balloon. We didn't have any of the normal balloons so we were using some that we bought at the shop. He fired one shot and it wouldn't burst the balloon and the gun jammed and I put my finger up to move the balloon at the same time as he shot.' Her finger was blown off. Incredibly, she continued the performance. 'We carried on. He didn't know – no idea.'

Eventually, they finished the act and Moira went to the hospital but the doctors told her there was nothing they could do. 'They said it would be like a cabbage so I said: "Take the damn thing off, it's no good to me!"' She shows me her stump, incongruous next to the long scarlet gel nails on every other finger. Sadly, Bobby had managed to blow off her ring finger – and her wedding and engagement ring with it. 'The ringmaster searched and about three or four days later, he came back with a diamond,' she says. They had the engagement ring rebuilt. She still has the original wedding ring, which bears the shape of the bullet.

As Bobby's wife, Moira was also expected to know

how to ride an elephant, and when visited by three sisters of the Fossett circus dynasty, she was obliged to teach them these skills. 'The youngest one couldn't ride,' she says. 'So Bobby's father said: "Get Moira in there and show her how to do it." I'd never been on an elephant's back in my life but because I was married to Bobby, it was expected that I would just do it and I had to pretend that I knew how to ride an elephant. I did it because I think I was more afraid of Bobby's father than I was of falling off the elephant.'

Unfortunately, not all her experiences with elephants were so positive. The couple were booked to go to Paris to perform for French President François Mitterrand, who was entertaining then Indian Prime Minister Rajiv Gandhi on a state visit in the 1980s. The elephants were adorned with 18-carat gold harnesses and Indian outfits for the occasion. They had rehearsed the show in the morning and everything had been perfect but as they began the performance and led the elephants in, watched by the heads of state, a dog ran under their elephant, Maureen. 'Maureen stepped back and on to my toe,' Moira recalls. As always, though, they continued the parade. 'When we got to the end and got the elephants comfortable and bedded down, I said: "We better go to the hospital now",' she says. A French doctor with a cigarette dangling from his mouth patched her up. 'The night before, when we arrived, they put us in a hotel you wouldn't put a dog in, so we slept in the car,' she adds.

'So when it came to rehearsal time the next morning, we said: "Unless you get us a decent hotel for us to wash and clean in, we're not doing the parade." So they put us in the George V on the Champs-Élysées. When we'd finished and we came back to have some sleep before we left the next day to go back to Scotland, we arrived in the George V and they've got Chinese rugs as you go in and my blood was dripping all the way up to the room. I said: "They'll never forget we were here!"'

CHAPTER 8

BOBBY NOW – PART TWO

When I first meet Bobby to interview him for this book, he has just woken from a nap. Since I last saw him in 2011, he has visibly aged. He seems very much an elderly grandfather now, whereas previously he seemed alert and in charge in the ring. He is ill at the moment and, in his blue and white checked shirt, matching socks and leather slippers, he looks his seventy-two years.

Bobby and his wife Moira had been happy to talk through their memories, but they are not so keen to discuss the more recent past. When I ask about the ADI footage and the trial, Bobby says: 'Why you gotta fetch it all up again?' When I put to them the allegations about cruelty to Anne, to give them the chance to tell their side of the story, they are visibly uncomfortable and defensive. Bobby even bristles at one point and I later receive an email from Moira accusing me of libelling them by asking difficult questions.

The couple remain furious – and unapologetic – about the release of the footage and the resulting court case. On Bobby's conviction, Moira says: 'He never did anything to start with. I think that was the worst part of the whole thing: that he genuinely didn't do anything wrong.' She adds: 'We should have got praise for keeping her [Anne] alive so long. She's not perfect but she's not dying.' When asked how she felt when I came to show her the footage, she replies: 'I'll never forget it. It was disbelief. It brought back the terrible memories of that boy [Steve Gills] hitting Mary Chipperfield's elephant. We never ever envisaged that that could happen to us. Never.' When convicted of allowing the groom to beat Anne, Bobby says he 'nearly died', adding: 'I'd done nothing, you know. How can I watch someone 24/7?' They both compare it to leaving a dog in kennels while on holiday. Bobby says: 'How many people go on holiday and put their dog in kennels? They don't expect somebody to come down and kick it, do they?'

Naturally they didn't enjoy the experience of being in court either. 'I was in the dock,' says Bobby. 'I've never been in court all my life, you know.' Moira adds: 'It was so horrible, as if we were murderers.' Bobby says that a 'bloody marvellous' security guard on the door

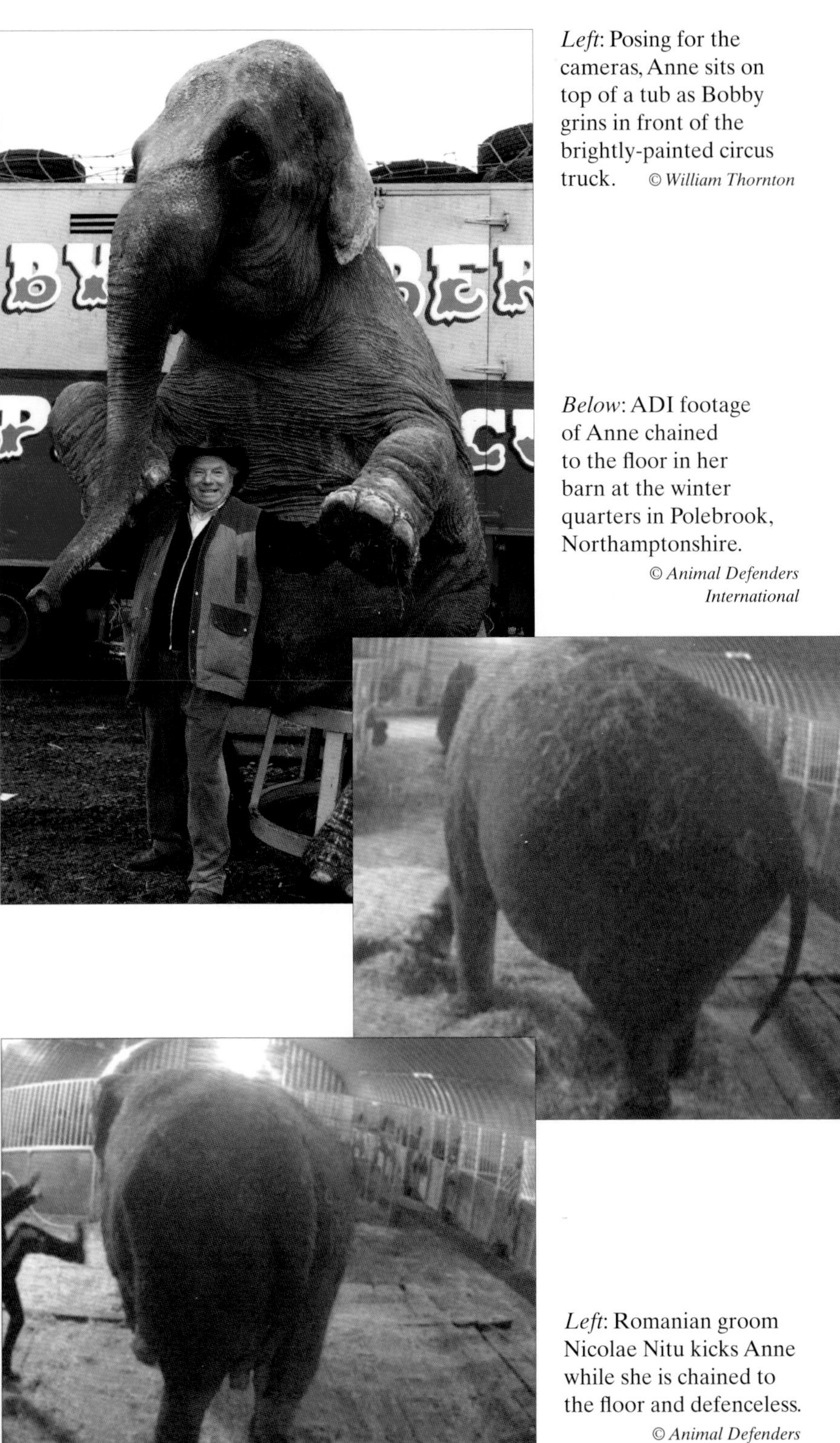

Left: Posing for the cameras, Anne sits on top of a tub as Bobby grins in front of the brightly-painted circus truck. *© William Thornton*

Below: ADI footage of Anne chained to the floor in her barn at the winter quarters in Polebrook, Northamptonshire.

© Animal Defenders International

Left: Romanian groom Nicolae Nitu kicks Anne while she is chained to the floor and defenceless.

© Animal Defenders International

Above: Anne at the Bobby Roberts Super Circus, her ankles in chains.

© Animal Defenders International

Below: Workers at the Bobby Roberts Super Circus use pliers to drag Anne by her ear when she refuses to return to her quarters. *© Animal Defenders International*

Left: She plays with her red ball as she celebrates her first Christmas at her new home in Longleat in December 2011.

Right: Enjoying herself in the mud as she poses outside Anne's Haven in August 2015.

Below: Costa, Coffee and Sugar the Anglo-Nubian goats keep Anne company in her new home in 2015.

Above left: A picture of health and vitality since leaving the circus, Anne shows how far she's come since her suffering.

Above right: Anne shows off the new-found strength in her trunk as her proud keepers look on in 2014.

Below: Happily rummaging around in a food bag in 2015.

of Northampton Crown Court summed it all up for him: 'He said: "We had two fellas in last week, they cut three children up in pieces, nobody wanted to know. And you came in and they're all over you, the press and everything."' The couple say they were hounded by the press the first day of the trial and a friend had to pick them up from outside court. The following day, the judge said that the pair had to be escorted out as a result. Bobby says that one of the photographers demanded a picture of them together, adding that he would 'hound you all your life' if they didn't agree to pose.

They also reveal that they wanted to appeal Bobby's sentence. 'Our barristers talked us out of it,' says Moira. 'For some reason both barristers thought we had got a good deal, but I wanted to appeal. We didn't have the money because we couldn't get legal aid.' Bobby adds: 'I had a lot of people say: "This is not right, you should appeal against it and do it." I said: "Let it drop."'

When I ask Moira about the fallout from the news story, she is visibly affected. 'That was the worst possible time,' she says. 'We'd been down at the farm [Polebrook] doing everything that needed to be done and when we came to Knutsford the family were all broken-hearted because there were hundreds of these protesters. Hundreds. And we had to get police protection to get to the trailer. Of course, we starved.' They then moved to Leigh in Lancashire, where Moira claims things were worse because the police didn't even control the protesters there. But the show went on and they continued performing. 'We carried on,' she says. 'We did go on, but what was it? To twenty people, twenty-five? We'd normally have had 400! It cost us everything we possessed to pay the artists, which we did, just to prove that we weren't afraid of people. It cost us a whole year of losing money.'

She says they received numerous death threats and were hounded by the media, and that they had to sell everything to pay their way. 'We sold everything we possessed, all our valuable things, jewellery... anything we had that was worth money. We sold assets from here – a bit of land here, bit of land there – and managed to end the season, albeit six weeks early, not owing anyone any money.' They remember vividly the protests that accompanied the circus. 'How many people were going to shoot us, how many people were going to go and get a gun,' she recalls. 'You haven't seen half of the letters we had. How many people were going to kidnap our kids.' Bobby adds: 'Some of the threats we had were terrible. We had the police outside for a month, driving up and down.' They also had to change all their phone numbers.

On the subject of Nicolae Nitu, the groom shown on the video meting out beatings to Anne, Moira says he'd been with the circus for a year and had been trained by Bobby. She describes him as 'kind', adding: 'That was why Bobby let him work on the elephants.' When I ask how she squares this with the harrowing footage she adds: 'I reckon that he was asked to do what he did. I've always said it. It's a well-known fact that Romanians will sell their grandma if they get enough money. Where did he get the money to leave? Where did he get the money to disappear in the middle of the night? We hadn't paid him.'

Her suggestion is clear: the groom was bribed to beat Anne and then paid off to disappear to avoid questions. So what were the intentions of whoever did this? She believes it was to ruin their business. 'You've got certain groups that no matter what we did or said they would still condemn us because of our lifestyle,' she says. 'Circus became a dirty word to those people.' Moira says she always sourced workers from the same village in Romania, which was where Nitu was from. She said at the time of the story that she felt personally responsible as she had hired him. 'I did interview him,' she says. 'He started on the tent. They always start on the tent unless they come to us as a groom. We'd see how they did.'

She says Nitu had wanted to work in the stables and had eventually been moved. She told me that they had employed him in April 2010 to look after Anne. Like Nitu, many of those working at the circus when I visited the first time were Eastern European migrants – presumably the low wages, difficult manual labour and long hours meant it was a job not many local people would want to do. They say that they paid Nitu

£8,000 a year – just over half of the annual salary for someone on minimum wage – and that he had been at the circus for about a year and couldn't speak English. The twenty-five-year-old – they showed me a copy of his ID – usually worked for the circus for about six months of the year and would then go back home for the winter.

Both she and Bobby claim that he never wore a hat or hoodie apart from when he beat Anne. Moira says: 'It was as if he knew he was on film. He was trying to hide his face.' She also remains convinced that there is something not quite right about the footage: 'Elephants never forget; they never forget a bad groom. If that boy was genuinely cruel to her, time in, time out, she wouldn't have let him near her. But with all the filming she had no problem with him coming near her. No problem at all.' She also insists that it was a plastic fork he was hitting her with and the couple claim the original footage was dubbed over to make it sound like metal thwacks.

Moira claims that they, like ADI, have been trying to find Nitu. 'We've been looking at circuses all over Europe,' she says. 'We needed an explanation about why he did what he did.' She says she gave his address to the police, adding: 'I gave them everything. We weren't afraid of finding him, we wanted to know.' She says circuses still report having seen him but 'the minute we get in touch he's either disappeared or we can't afford the money to fly wherever he is'.

I point out to them that although Nitu is clearly the guilty party in terms of the beating, Bobby was the one who was convicted for how she was kept. When I ask if it was wrong that Anne was kept permanently chained to the floor, Moira says: 'I agree there' and says Bobby blames himself for leaving Nitu – 'He had many a sleepless night because he left the boy, which was wrong. He should have supervised him, there's no doubt about it. It keeps us awake at night.' When I ask what they expected Anne's normal routine to be while in Nitu's care, she replies: 'It was winter time so she wouldn't have been taken out in the field if there was any frost or anything. The only exercise she had was what we thought she was having, which is getting loose in the stables. There was plenty of room inside the barn for her to exercise. We always have a ring in for training the animals anyway so she had access to that and we thought that's what was happening. It should have been twice [a day she was let out].'

Bobby insists that he has never used violence to train his animals. 'I have loads and loads of people saying you must beat them,' he says. 'But if you beat them they won't come to you, they won't love you. They don't come when you shout at them in the field and that is the thing that people get the wrong idea [about. They say] that's how I thought you did it and it's not at all.'

He compares training elephants to training any animal. 'It's like that dog out there,' he says, gesturing towards the family Cane Corso, an Italian Mastiff. 'It's half-human. People don't believe it, but that dog will do anything and it's just a dog that come one day.' Moira adds: 'Anne was human. How soon before they stop people keeping dogs? It's only because the Queen's got so many horses and the racing world is such a multimillionaire organisation that horses are not picked on.' Bobby picks up the theme: 'How many grooms has the Queen got looking after horses? Does that mean that she's got to be there all the time looking at them?'

Moira says that Bobby's skill with the elephants is all down to his voice. 'I always thought that Bobby was that bit different and he was,' she says. 'He had a rapport with the animals, particularly the elephants. Something different that other elephant trainers didn't have. I don't know what it was but he could speak to his animals. He still does.' She stresses that Bobby was never cruel to his animals. 'I never, ever believed that anyone could accuse Bobby Roberts of being cruel,' she insists. 'It was the farthest thing from his mind. He never had a cruel streak. Never.'

She stresses that Bobby said he educated, rather than trained his elephants. 'Bobby always said you educate an animal the same as you educate a child,' she says. 'It'll follow you. It'll not learn if you don't teach it.' She also insists that he didn't use physical punishment on them. 'I think Bobby chastised the elephants more than scolded them but with his voice because his voice was his secret. He didn't have to use a whip, it was his voice.'

When I ask Bobby how he would train an elephant, he says: 'You take it and educate it and walk it round and you walk it into these tricks when they're babies. It's like a child. You put the food on a fork and put it in the child's mouth: after a bit it gets used to it and does it itself. It's the same thing [with] elephants when they all walk in a line holding the other one's tail. They don't do that. You have to hold it and after a bit – it might take a day, two days, a month – it'll just walk and do it.' He adds that the elephants are trained one at a time, and then another and another is added until they perform together. 'Soon as they got used to holding the other one's tail they'd all follow each other, you know.'

The couple say the elephants loved to perform and would drag the tub to the door because they wanted to go when it came round to touring season. (At this point, Moira rebukes me for a charge I didn't make: 'And you say they don't want to be in the circus. It was so plain to see.')

Anne was well used to travelling by train when it was the customary way to transport elephants and they would parade through towns. Bobby says they loved visiting different places on the train, but he was never too happy when they arrived back at the local station: 'They used to come out of the station and they'd look round like this and just go. They were back in the stables when we got back here. They went through everywhere because they knew the road. They'd go through the barbed wire fences and take the lot with them. I couldn't keep up with them.'

I ask about the allegations that Anne wasn't receiving medication for her arthritis. Moira says that they fed her aspirin for years but didn't realise there were better medicines they should have been giving her. They claim they followed veterinary advice throughout but acknowledge the effect the RSPCA-recommended pain relief had on her. 'It was like a miracle when they put her on the new medicine,' Moira says. 'We thought that we were going to lose her when the vet saw her. We always knew [she was in pain] but we thought we treated her for the pain and she didn't cry or anything and elephants can cry.'

The couple also deny a life of performing in the circus is connected to Anne's arthritis. 'I don't believe that,' says Bobby. 'I mean, they stand up and pull trees down in the jungle, they stand up to breed, and sitting on a tub there's no weight on her legs. They're sitting on the tub. No, it's old age. We all get stiff back and arthritis and things like that.'

They do not accept that she stereotyped – 'bobbed', as they call it – when she lived with them, though the footage captured by ADI shows her constantly stereotyping. They also vehemently deny that Bobby has ever used a bullhook on the elephants. When I ask them about it and ask them what they call bullhooks, Moira says icily: 'Nothing. Because Bobby didn't know what an ankus was. In the court he had no idea. He's never used one.' Bobby says of the prosecuting barrister who cross-examined him in court: 'She was getting annoyed because I thought it was an anchor off a boat. I'd never heard of it.'

I tell them that I was shown a picture of Bobby with a bullhook that had been sent to Longleat by a member of the public, though I have no way of verifying the photo. They say this is 'impossible'. Bobby says: 'One hundred per cent you've never seen a picture of me with a hook or an anchor or whatever.' Moira's response is: 'It was something that Bobby's always abhorred but we knew they were perfectly legal in a zoo.' Bobby adds that his voice was all he needed: 'I just always said if you couldn't hold it [the elephant] with your tongue, unless you got their four legs tied up you couldn't handle them and when I shouted that was enough.'

Bobby says he often used a walking stick for the lead elephant to hold on to. He also says he used a whip for cracking, but not to hit the elephants. To make his point, he returns to his methods of training elephants. 'It's like people say with a horse: "You have to beat it." I said: "If you beat it, it goes down the other end of the field. It's not going to come to you, is it? And the first chance it gets, it's off,"' he says. 'People used to say to me by law you're supposed to have a hook but I never did. The elephant weighs three tonnes and it doesn't matter what you do unless it's with you.'

When I ask about Chris Draper from Born Free's allegation that Bobby used an implement in his hand during the move, the couple are apoplectic. Bobby says he had a spanner to undo her shackles and also says he had a Leatherman, a kind of Swiss Army knife, but he denies using them on Anne, and he sighs: 'They don't half come up with some things.' Moira later points out that the whole move was filmed and no one had produced any evidence of him using an implement. The couple say they were both apprehensive about Longleat's decision to use bullhooks on Anne. Moira says: 'We saw them hanging in the thing and I said: "They're not going to use them, are they, Bob?" They said they had to have them. We said: "We'd prefer if you didn't use them on Anne."'

Bobby and Moira remain in two minds about Anne's life at Longleat. They are pleased that she is on her own as they claim she hated other elephants – a controversial subject, given many animal rights groups think she needs other elephants. 'Anne didn't like the other elephants,' Moira says, 'and as she got older, they used to knock her down and we had to take her away. That's why I know she's happy where she is and if they ever say that they're bringing in more elephants I'd think we'd have a lot to say about that.' They insist she was bullied and her feeding had to take place at a different time from the other elephants. Asked how

Anne got on with Beverly and Janie, Moira responds in a deadpan fashion: 'She didn't. We used to have to keep them apart. If we thought they were going to pick on her we'd take her away and we fed her separately otherwise they stole all her food. She was a slow eater.' Anne was wider and shorter than the other elephants, a runt compared to Beverly and Janie, who were both big elephants, she says. Her companions died in 2001, Beverly the victim of an apparent poisoning as already mentioned, but asked how Janie died, Moira adds: 'She just pined [for Beverly], I think. And that left us with Anne, who didn't pine.'

The pair are not thrilled by the goats Anne has for company – which Moira says 'smell' – and would prefer her to have a pony, but they were happier that she was being looked after by Andy Hayton, who was trained by the Chipperfields when they were based at Longleat. Neither, however, believes that Anne likes her new home at Longleat. Moira adds to Bobby: 'Truthfully, she knew that you didn't like her in a cage.' He responds: 'No, I didn't.'

Both really struggle with the new husbandry system Longleat uses called 'protected contact', which prevents direct human interaction with Anne. Bobby is visibly confused when told about protected contact. 'What do you mean, she's not allowed human contact?' he says. When I explain the training system that teaches her to lift her legs, for example, by teaching her the association, he replies: 'They only had to say: "Lift your leg up, Anne."' Moira adds: 'They call it Anne's Haven. How can they call it a haven? I'd bring her home tomorrow if they would let us.'

They also accuse Longleat of breaking its promises and using Anne for publicity, and Moira describes her fury when a Longleat press officer said they had 'rescued' Anne. 'We agree with how Longleat are looking after her, we just feel that they let us down. We don't feel like they did us proud. They betrayed us, didn't they, by allowing the press to say things? They didn't rescue her.'

Moira is keen to establish that Anne was not taken from them, and that they willingly gave her away. 'We gave her to them,' she says. 'We didn't sell her. We had no intentions of making money out of her. We just want her to be content and she's not content now because she likes to talk to people. She missed people more than another elephant.' She is adamant: 'We could've sold her a thousand times over to circuses around the world, knowing that she'd been trained by Bobby.' I ask for how much, to which Bobby replies £100,000. Moira is quick to add that they never put a price on her. Bobby also reveals that he has been offered work with elephants since. 'I've had no end of people phone up: "Will you come and train some elephants?" I said no.'

The couple say they tried to retire Anne in 2009. Moira recalls that they had a meeting with the Born Free Foundation about where to send Anne: 'We called these so-called absolutely wonderful people, Born Free. We said to them it was time for Anne to retire but we'd have to be very careful where she went.' The charity accuse the pair of demanding money for Anne, something Moira says is 'lies'. Whatever happened, the talks stalled and Anne remained where she was for another two years.

They are angry that people think that they made money out of the animals. 'People think that we're making an absolute fortune,' Moira says. 'They never stopped to think that we had the animals because we cared for them. We loved the animals and we wanted them with us.' Bobby adds: 'The people who didn't have the animals, they didn't have to buy hay for 'em and they got all the good grounds. You'd get people complaining about the animals so we'd have to go into a farmer's field or something, you know.'

'It was a way of life we had,' continues Moira, 'it was never a way of earning money. People thought you were millionaires. They maybe [were] in Bobby's dad's day.' Bobby adds: 'When it was seven and six to come in, they made a lot of money. That's how this place [the winter quarters] was built.'

Moira says the footage of Anne being beaten and the resulting media coverage and court case ruined their lives not just emotionally, but also financially. 'We only live on our pension now, that's all we've got,' she reveals. 'We've sold everything.'

Though they plead poverty, it is difficult to see them as paupers. Their main car is a Mercedes-Benz estate, with a personalised number plate including the letters 'BR' for Bobby Roberts. The rest of the family drive Mercedes' and an Audi. And the couple, both in their seventies, fiddle with an iPad as we talk. Despite this, Moira says they get by on odd jobs but later tells me they have no income at all. She says Bobby makes harnesses and leather mobile phone covers to sell, which he shows me. 'We're left with what we stand up in, which is fine,' she adds. I ask if she ever wanted a real house. 'I did have ambitions to have a house,' she admits. 'Those days have passed.' I ask whether it's a connection with history to live in the trailer, but she rejects that suggestion: 'You get to the point where you say you live in a caravan and they think you're a gypsy.'

They reveal that they plan to get back into the circus industry at some point in the future. As of 2015, Bobby's conviction is removed from his record, giving them a clean slate to bring the circus back. 'We're not on the road because of lack of money,' Moira says. 'What happened four years ago just absolutely finished us. Our children want to go on the road again. My son-in-law, my daughter, they all want to go out again. I'll try. It's not even just us, it's the kids, it's in their blood.' She says they still have the material they need though she cautions that to start the season they'd need at least £65,000 up front to cover tax, insurance and maintenance. And their family want to join them. Their son, another Bobby Roberts, forty-two, is a clown who lives in Scotland. Their grandchildren are keen to get back on the road. Bobby himself on many occasions has vowed never to give up. 'I've seen old circus people retire and they die real quick,' he has said in the past.

Their only remaining animals are two horses and four miniature Falabella horses, some of which are with their granddaughter Summer, twenty-three, who is on tour with Zippo's Circus as I write. The tenth generation of the family to enter the business, she is keen to be back on the road with her family, according to her grandmother. Summer's act, which, she directs herself, is called the 'Liberty Horses', which Moira explains involves six horses galloping round the ring. She has another act with a big horse and a tiny pony called Big and Little and she also rides dressage on an Andalusian stallion. Moira is gushing in her admiration. 'She's Bobby repeated,' she says. 'We skipped a generation. Our own two children loved the animals but they haven't got that certain something. Summer lives and breathes the horses. That's what Bobby's so pleased about: someone following in his footsteps.'

Asked whether they could bring back the wild animals of Bobby's father's day, Moira is realistic. She says: 'I don't honestly believe that we could bring back the wild animals. And I never look on animals as wild, don't get me wrong: I refuse to believe elephants are wild, they're domesticated.' Bobby adds: 'I don't take none of them wild when you brought 'em up from a baby. Chipperfields had more tigers born in the circus than there was in the wild. They had them everywhere – in the cupboards and everywhere.' They say that people ride camels in Egypt and elephants in India, and Bobby says that people want to see circuses with wild animals return: 'You go to a circus and they say: "Oh, there's no lions in it!" And I say: "I know, why isn't there no lions?" The thing of going to the show is to see them do that loop-the-loop, that's the idea of going.'

He was astonished to see a trapeze artist wearing a wire called a lunge to protect her from falling. 'It's the same thing – you went to the circus for the thrills. I went to the circus the other day and the girl's got a lunge on. I said: "Look at that." Years ago, nobody ever had a lunge for some of these things. Then health and safety come along.' Moira agrees. She says that the public consultation on wild animals in circuses was not a true reflection of the public's beliefs: 'That's only a tiny minority who make themselves heard. It's alright saying the majority want rid of us but how many people did they speak to, to get their figures?'

Bobby thinks that circus animals are victims of the health and safety culture that pervades the UK. 'Here used to be the world championship conker,' he says. 'They stopped it, health and safety. It's ridiculous. Kids have played with conkers for years. They did have to have a hard hat, glasses, gloves and things, and then they went and they just stopped.' He remembers one particular upsetting incident from his time on the road. 'I think it was the very first Children in Need and we wasn't far from the studios and somebody had offered £10,000 to stroke or touch the elephant or something and they wouldn't allow it. It was the charity that lost out... from health and safety.'

I then ask them if they think they've been left behind by changing times. Moira says: 'Times change, course they change, and we tried to keep up with them. When you'd been doing something that didn't do the animals any harm that you'd been doing for as many years as you can remember, why stop doing it?'

Bobby's nostalgia is evident from the fact he still visits circuses. 'It's sad, you know,' he says. 'She don't, but I go to see all the circuses.' Moira adds: 'It's in his blood, he can't help it. I get too upset.' When I ask Bobby what he thinks of them, he pauses. 'Half of them have got no animals and the ones that do...' He tails off. Asked about Cirque du Soleil, which doesn't feature animals, he is less than impressed. 'A bit boring, innit?' he says. 'Some clever things in it, but it's the money again. You can do anything if you've got money, can't you?'

But he seems encouraged by Tommy Chipperfield's Big Cat act, which was introduced in 2014. Asked if they remain friendly with the Chipperfields, he says: 'Yeah, of course. All true circus people.' 'Not many what they call true circus people left,' says Moira. They are quick, however, to say they didn't know Mary Chipperfield, who is from another branch of the family.

Asked if life has improved since the fuss surrounding Anne has died down, Moira shakes her head. 'It's been a living hell ever since,' she admits. 'It's only having such a good family that's...' she tails off. 'You want to think that the last years of your life will be comfortable, that you've nothing to feel guilty about, but all we feel is guilt. In some way we took away Anne's last years of life with us by giving her away. We thought it was going to be better for her but I don't think it is. The neighbours used to look forward to elephants being in the field at the front, now they see a field of rotten hay.'

Bobby insists that Anne would know him now if he went to visit her. 'I'd think nothing about walking straight in and she'd come up to me and she'd squeak,' he says. 'I've seen elephants that I've had no contact with for years and years and soon as I walked up, they're just like babies.' He also says that Anne enjoyed performing. 'It's funny, they all liked to be centre of attention. I bet if I walked up there now she'd do most of the tricks.' Moira agrees: 'She hasn't changed. She knows us, she'll never forget because they don't forget.'

Bobby adds: 'If you could ask her, would she turn round and say she'd like to be back with us? I think she would. The number of people who've said that it was cruel to take the elephant away. I said they didn't take her away – I gave her [away] because I thought it was a better home for her. But they said she must have missed the circus.' He becomes nostalgic. 'When you play that "St Louis Blues", they was off. You could be anywhere in the world and they would be standing by the back door and it didn't matter what language they spoke but they knew when they said Bobby Roberts and that music played they were gone to work. They loved to work, and they loved to please you.'

I leave in two minds. It's easy to see the Robertses as an elderly couple who belong to a different era and were left behind by changing times. The other circuses spotted the warning signs and adapted, but they kept Anne going. Public opinion made them fair game for animal rights groups to target and they would have been naïve not to realise the potential consequences. In many ways it's easy to see them as the victims of circumstance, simply unable or unwilling to accept the change in mentality that left them behind.

Bobby, a man feted for his elephant husbandry, was nothing without the animals that had defined him. Whether or not he did a lot of the things he is accused of will probably never be known. Both he and his wife seem to have genuine affection for the animals they shared their lives with. And though Moira is sharp and all too savvy, it's not hard to understand why, living as they have in the firing line for so many years. Looking back on previous interviews the couple – and especially

Moira – have given, I am struck by how some of the phrases are rolled out time and time again almost verbatim. All too often her protestations of love for Anne and the circus and denigration of animal rights groups and protesters sound rehearsed. But I remind myself again that they have lived under siege for so long that they must have simply become accustomed to handing out the same replies.

I struggle to believe they're the evil monsters they're often painted as. And even if we do accept that Bobby mistreated the elephants, it is of course a further jump to prove that he ever did so knowingly or meant them harm. For so many years, as Britain's last circus elephant, Anne had been the unwitting pawn in a battle between animal rights campaigners and an industry steeped in tradition. It is clear which side won in the end, but I can't help but feel a pang of sympathy as I pull out of the drive, leaving the grandparents and their young grandchildren playing in the yard.

CHAPTER 9

MOIRA AND BOBBY ROBERTS GO ON TRIAL CHARGED WITH ANIMAL CRUELTY

In November 2011, seven months after Anne was rehomed, the Crown Prosecution Service (CPS) announced that it was taking the Robertses to court. They were jointly charged with causing unnecessary suffering to Anne by chaining her to the floor at all times, failing to prevent her groom from beating her and failing to ensure her needs were met. All three of the offences were brought under the Animal Welfare Act 2006. It was the first time a circus had been prosecuted under the act, which replaced legislation originally drawn up in 1911, and it was hailed as a 'landmark' case by ADI. The organisation had begun the process as a private prosecution in April 2011 but the CPS later agreed to take it on given the 'public concern' about the case.

Opening the case for the prosecution, CPS barrister Helen Law played the ADI footage dating from between 21 January and 15 February 2011, which showed Anne being stabbed with a pitchfork, beaten and kicked by her groom, Nicolae Nitu. The court was told that Bobby failed to provide any pain relief to her to alleviate the crippling arthritis that caused her to drag her leg behind her. The Robertses insisted she often refused to take it but they tried to give it to her. After she was given it at the RSPCA's direction, she showed a 'significant improvement', the court was told. The footage also showed her constantly chained by one front leg and one hind leg in the squalid metal compound she called home. Bobby was shown supervising the swapping of the chains from one leg to the other without allowing her to be unchained for even a few moments. He later said he 'couldn't explain' why he saw her chained and did nothing about it. The footage also showed a particularly heartbreaking moment when Anne reached out to him with her trunk and he gave it a sharp kick. 'The elephant moves her trunk over inquiringly and is rebuffed with a kick,' Miss Law said. Despite his professed devotion to the elephant, who Moira described at one point as 'like a child' to the couple, Bobby entered the barn only four times during the three-and-a-half week filming period.

He said in court that this was due to health problems. Moira, meanwhile, did not enter the barn once.

Bobby denied all the charges and insisted that all members of his staff were adequately trained. He said Nitu did not follow his orders and said that he was unable to supervise him due to health problems that stopped him working in the barn as much as he usually did. When asked whether he always supervised workers, he said: 'You do get a bit complacent. You do think that the people are doing the job that they're supposed to be doing.' He added: 'I did see her chained but it didn't enter my mind that she hadn't been loose.' Bobby denied claims by the prosecutor that he had instructed his grooms just to change the chains rather than let her free. He replied: 'No, I told them to let her loose.' But Miss Law told the court that the grooms were 'plainly inadequately trained'. 'The footage shows a near-on absolute lack of supervision from Bobby Roberts,' she told the court. 'Moira Roberts never enters the barn. Whatever Bobby Roberts' health, there were other people on this site – his wife, his daughter – who could have gone to supervise these grooms. There is no suggestion that anybody else was asked to do so.'

Miss Law also said that Nitu had been trained to hit Anne and to keep her chained to the ground. 'Bobby Roberts was quite happy to authorise casual violence towards the elephant,' she said. She added: 'A lot of violence took place in front of other staff members, which suggests the violence was endemic.' She also said that Anne swaying back and forth was a sign of her boredom and frustration. When the creature was chained, she 'didn't have the ability to move or exhibit normal behaviour patterns' and could be seen to sway – what is known in the industry as 'stereotypic behaviour'. 'This is a sign of distress,' Miss Law suggested.

Animal welfare experts told the court that Anne suffered almost constantly while she was at the circus. Donald Broom, professor of animal welfare at Cambridge University, who analysed the footage for the prosecution, explained how elephants – like humans – display abnormal behaviour when experiencing prolonged stress. This includes 'stereotypies' – repetitive movements with no discernible function. When Anne was chained up alone, the video footage showed her bobbing her head up and down, moving her trunk, lifting a front leg and swaying from side to side. She repeated the same three- or four-second sequence of movements until something 'interesting' happened, such as a human arriving or being fed.

Professor Broom told the court: 'In my analysis she is showing this stereotypy for about 90 per cent of the time. Normally if one is shown for more than 5 per cent of the time we would say there is a serious problem. It is an indicator of poor welfare.' He said constant chaining, which was not in accordance with the Association of

Circus Providers' standards, could alone have caused the stereotypy. Anne did not have sufficient space and ability to move and that was a 'very serious problem', Professor Broom said, adding that tethering would also increase the pain she was suffering from arthritis. According to him, her behaviour indicated long periods of poor welfare from tethering and lack of social companionship, and this was 'the cause of the greatest suffering for the elephant, more than the hitting'. He said that elephants feel pain in a similar way to humans and respond to it by flinching or moving away from the source: 'We know for example they respond to insect bites and being pricked, as well as to more substantial blows,' he said. 'The fact they have thick skin does not mean that they do not feel pain.'

When Bobby (then seventy years old) took the stand, he said that he was 'disgusted' by the footage of Anne being beaten by her groom, and that Nitu's treatment of the elephant was 'disgraceful'. He told District Judge David Chinery that he didn't know the groom was abusing Anne and that she was kept chained to the ground all day. He also told the court that had he known what was happening to her, he would have done something about it. 'It's disgraceful, disgusting. I can't tell you what I would have done. The police would have been involved. Still now when I think about it, it goes through me. I just can't believe it.' Had he actually seen Nitu strike Anne with a pitchfork, he insisted: 'He would have got fired straight away. There is no second chance and I'd want to know why. I might have hit him with the pitchfork.'

Nitu, Bobby said, had not followed his instructions. But he was unable to explain why he did not act when he found Anne chained up. He admitted that she would be chained up at times but said his instructions were to let her loose behind an electric fence in a cordoned-off area of the barn when possible or, if the weather was good, to take her to a field outside. He told the court: 'I didn't know that she'd not been off, I was disgusted that we didn't know. Do you think I would have let it go on if I'd have known anything about it?' However, it was mentioned in court that after the footage was first made public in the paper, police and the RSPCA visited Anne's home and found that her enclosure had been significantly altered. She was unchained and in an area of the barn deep with straw and cordoned off by an electric fence. Miss Law said this was because Bobby knew keeping her chained was 'not permissible under the required standards'. When asked whether he ever allowed the use of any implements or weapons on any of his animals, Bobby said: 'I would never ever have let anybody touch anything.' He said that he tried to give her aspirin to treat her arthritis, but she refused to take it. 'I put the medicine in apples, bananas. She'd take it for about three days and then she would stop,' he told the court. Bizarrely, he also told the court that instead he would give her brandy if she was 'off-colour'. He also said he sometimes fed her candy floss. Moira denied having any involvement in the care of the elephant or the training of staff and denied owning Anne.

When asked about kicking Anne, Bobby told the court he 'flicked' her trunk with his foot because he didn't want her to spoil his suit. When I asked him about it at the circus, he categorically denied that he had kicked her. He told the court from the stand: 'I would never hit her, I would command her by tongue. I might shout at her sometimes but that was just so she could hear what I said. When the video shows me flick my foot at her trunk that was because I was wearing a suit and I wanted her away from it. She's taught not to put her trunk on people, and elephants leave a smell on a suit. I would not normally be [there] in a suit but I was told something had disturbed her while I was not there so I came in. I've known Anne since I was ten or eleven. She belonged to my father and uncle before me. We used to have two more elephants, but by 2011 she was the only one left. She is sixty now and is the oldest elephant in captivity.'

He said that he always ensured that she was seen by a vet and that she was normally chained up at night or when washed, but usually unchained during the day. He told the court that the grooms he had employed were all from the same Romanian village. 'I had never seen that [the beating] being done and I certainly didn't tell them to do it,' he added. He told the court that he talked to

Anne's head keeper at Longleat 'every week' to tell him how to handle her.

The court also heard sentimental details about Anne's life from her owner. Bobby said that he missed her company: 'There's something missing now she's gone. I used to watch her from the house when she was in the pen and I'd see her go over to my caravan because she knew Moira was in there,' he said. The court heard Bobby treated Anne 'like family'. He said: 'If I went to Longleat now and I stood at the end of the field she would know that I was there. She'd make a noise on the floor and her ears would flap out. Then she'd start to scream and shout if I called her a good girl.'

Former circus staff also testified that Bobby had never told them to keep Anne chained and had not seen him treat his animals cruelly. A former ringmaster at the circus, Derfel Williams, said Bobby had treated his animals better than humans – 'Mr Roberts had relationships with his animals like people have with their families.' When asked what he thought of Bobby kicking Anne's trunk, he said: 'That was a get-off sort of flick. I wouldn't even call it a kick. The animals were treated better than the humans. It was animals first at all times.' A former groom, Anthony Hall, who worked at the winter quarters, told the court he had never been told to keep the elephant permanently chained. He said: 'She wasn't always chained and Bobby didn't ask me that either.' He added that he was shown how to wash and muck out the elephant and how to change the chains. Mr Hall told the court he was never instructed to strike or use implements on the animal. 'I don't think I would be stood here if I had,' he said.

Jon Cracknell from Longleat was also called as a defence witness, something he said his bosses were none too happy about. He said Anne was in very good condition for her age and told the court the couple regularly contacted Longleat to check on her progress. 'Mr Roberts does care about Anne,' he said. 'These are not the actions of someone for whom she was out of sight, out of mind. I don't feel Mr Roberts is someone who is the cruel example of the circus industry that is being made out in the newspapers.' Giving evidence, Jon said guidelines stated that elephants should be chained for no more than three hours in a twenty-four-hour period. 'Being chained up for long periods could well adversely affect arthritis,' he told the court.

I, unfortunately, was not allowed to cover the case as I had been called as a witness due to my role in bringing it to light and confronting the Robertses. I was asked to give a police statement of my conversations with the Robertses and was told that I would be called by the prosecution. The prosecution decided not to use my evidence, but the defence decided that they would. So I came to court, though it was all in vain because they agreed my evidence at the last moment and I wasn't called.

The court also heard some interesting detail about how ADI managed to capture the shocking footage. Robert Brooks, the organisation's investigations manager who uses a false surname, said he had entered the farm's premises under a fence in a covert night operation, and placed a camera in a hole in the barn directly behind Anne. In tense scenes, he was asked whether the situation was fabricated to get publicity for ADI, but replied: 'Certainly not.' He also denied that Nitu was a plant by ADI to get Anne out of the circus. The campaign group was incensed when the Robertses' lawyers referred to them as 'extremists', leading to rebukes from the CPS and the judge. Jan Creamer said at the time: 'It is a pity the defence team has reduced itself to name-calling and unfounded allegations to smear the reputation of ADI investigators, whose evidence has been used by courts and governments around the world.'

At the end of the four-day trial, on 23 November 2012, the judge said he was satisfied that Anne had been chained for an 'excessive' period and had suffered as a result. He said that Bobby was aware that she was chained and had never asked for her to be unchained. He also remarked on the occasion that Bobby actually supervised the changing over of the chain from one of her legs to the other – without even giving her time to stretch her legs. He said that Bobby saw Anne in chains but 'for reasons which he cannot explain' did nothing about it. He accused Bobby of failing to supervise the groom properly and said it was clear Nitu was acting under instructions to keep Anne chained but he told the circus owner: 'The real cruelty was inflicted by your groom, who acted without your knowledge.' He said he accepted that Anne's treatment did not represent Bobby's normal level of care for animals under his control. 'You are a man who has not previously been convicted of any offence and it is to your credit that you have cared for and managed animals for the greater part of your seventy years without criticism from any quarter,' he said. He added that Bobby's offences had been at the lower end of the scale and said that he had not personally been cruel to her.

In sympathetic remarks at the conclusion of the case, Judge Chinery said Bobby had an 'exemplary record of animal husbandry' and had 'suffered enough punishment over the last eighteen months'. He accepted that the couple had a 'deep love for and care very much about the animals under their control' and added that he believed Bobby 'would not abuse an animal or use a weapon on any animal under his control'. He described Bobby as a man 'whom I found to be a witness of truth, an engaging man whose love for his animals (and his family) was apparent from the beginning. His distress at seeing the video footage of the groom striking Anne was both genuine and very moving. He has devoted his whole life to the circus, performing from the age of four, and clearly has many talents.'

Judge Chinery continued: 'Bobby Roberts impressed me both as a man and as a witness. He has remained calm and conducted himself with great dignity in the face of opprobrium.' In his findings, he concluded that for 'most of the time Bobby Roberts has been responsible for the care of his animals they have been looked after and cared for to a high physical standard such that no responsible person has had cause to complain about the standard of physical care afforded to them.' He described the moment Bobby kicked Anne as a 'casual flick' to protect his clothes and said others, including Jon at Longleat, had struggled to give her medication for her arthritis. He also revealed that he had asked the police to 'ensure the safety' of the couple after members of the public emailed the court threatening the pair.

His words would have been difficult for ADI to listen to, convinced as they were of Bobby's violent attitude towards animals. But the judge had far harsher words for the campaign group. He was highly critical of them for releasing the footage to the media rather than the police. This, he argued, led to the couple being 'tried by the public' and their grandchildren being 'ostracized by their peers'. He also criticised ADI for 'sitting on' the evidence for two months, meaning Anne was left in her situation. However, he said that ADI would probably argue that their actions had the 'desired effect', and had they notified the RSPCA, the animal charity would have been able to ensure Anne got to a place of safety and there would have been no need to bring a 'costly' trial. He went on to suggest that Anne's welfare was only part of ADI's objective and said that they had a 'wider agenda' to secure a ban on wild animals in circuses. His comments on their investigator, Robert Brooks, were scathing. He said that the court must treat his evidence 'with caution' as he worked for ADI and was 'somewhat circumspect' with the detail he gave in his evidence. At one point during the trial, it was even suggested that Nitu was 'an employee planted by ADI' – something Jan Creamer denied 'vehemently'. Ultimately, the judge accepted that ADI were telling the truth on this matter.

Despite his sympathetic words for Bobby, the judge did concede that 'the tethering of Anne with the chains for long periods of time would have resulted in increased suffering to her', adding: 'the fact that on several occasions Bobby did not tell Nitu to unchain Anne and the fact that at one point he assisted the groom in changing the chains leads me to conclude that the groom was acting under his instructions.' He also said: 'During the time that Anne was chained she did not have sufficient space and ability to move as required by good practice and this I regard as a very serious problem. As a result, Anne was unable to exhibit normal behaviour patterns, again as required by good practice. This also gave rise to stereotypy.'

Judge Chinery concluded: 'Bobby Roberts, by his own admission, failed to exercise sufficient supervision over his groom during the period in question thus resulting in the physical abuse, the excessive chaining and the lack, at times, of sufficient bedding to enable Anne to lie down when she was chained during the day.' He also criticised Nitu's 'acts of extreme cruelty to a defenceless animal'.

He found Bobby guilty of animal cruelty, but didn't jail him or fine him for his role in her suffering; he didn't even prevent him from keeping animals. Instead, Bobby was given a conditional discharge, despite the maximum sentence for each charge being a £20,000 fine and six months in jail. The judge then discharged him on the condition he did not commit any further offence for three years. Explaining his decision, he said: 'As a result of what has happened your business is effectively at an end. You have lost everything which you have built up over the last five decades. I am told that you have no funds at all.' The judge said it would be 'disproportionate' to ban him from keeping animals.

Moira, then seventy-five, did not give evidence but supplied a letter from her GP. She was cleared of the same charges after the judge ruled that she was not an owner of Anne and was therefore not responsible for her care. She sobbed in the dock as she was cleared and remained next to her husband after being told she could leave. He wiped away tears from his face with a handkerchief as he was then sentenced. When the trial ended, the pair left the court without commenting.

The sentence appalled many. ADI chief Jan Creamer called it 'derisory' and said it sent out the wrong message to other animal owners and circuses. She said at the time: 'Despite the considerable suffering caused to Anne the elephant, the sentencing meted out to Mr Roberts is derisory and provides no faith that the Animal Welfare Act can protect animals in circuses. People should be held responsible for the day-to-day experiences of their animals.' She also said the dramatic improvement in Anne's health following proper treatment for her arthritis at Longleat proved that she'd not been cared for properly. 'How well she is now in comparison shows you that she suffered over a long period of time,' she said. The animal rights campaign group were especially angry as they had held it up as a test case because it was the first trial of circus owners under the 'duty of care' component of the Animal Welfare Act, which states that owners can be held responsible for what happens to their animals. ADI, who secured the three previous circus cruelty convictions in the UK, also spent vast sums of money on the prosecution and ended the year in debt.

Sadly, there was no prosecution for any of the offences against the other animals. Jan Creamer said: 'They base it on the species. When the crown lawyers looked at it, it was decided that a lot of charges would be dropped in order to streamline it and focus on Anne. It's the same thing that happened with Mary Chipperfield.' This meant that there were no prosecutions in relation to the camel and miniature ponies. She added: 'Personally, we wouldn't agree with it, but often what happens is that people look at the big iconic animals and focus on them, but horses, dogs and small animals suffer as much. It's whether they can feel pain and fear and distress and all species can feel pain and fear and distress. Certainly you can see from the behaviour of those animals how frightened they were and how they suffered but those are the decisions that prosecutors make.' ADI co-founder Tim Phillips added: 'The evidence was there but animal cruelty is up there with stealing a bicycle. That's the unfortunate reality: we're constantly trying to push the status of animals up but they're not there yet.' Luckily for them, the public disagrees and public pressure can be brought to bear very heavily, as it was with Bobby Roberts.

The CPS, on the other hand, were pleased to have got a guilty verdict and that justice had been done. Following the conclusion of the trial, Richard Crowley, deputy chief prosecutor at CPS East Midlands who brought the case, said that the treatment of Anne had been upsetting to many. 'Bobby Roberts had clear responsibilities for this elephant's welfare, which he wilfully had not just breached his professional obligations towards Anne, but had been neglectful and abusive to a criminal degree. He gave instructions for Anne to be chained and took no action to prevent the beatings she had received, failing to provide any training or supervision for the staff member responsible for her,' he said.

Nitu is thought to have fled to his native Romania. ADI said that they went to his mother's house and were told that he was working as a builder. But he cannot be extradited to the UK to face charges as an arrest warrant cannot be issued for animal cruelty. 'We tracked him down afterwards to where he was,' said Jan. 'He'd gone home to his mother and we sent people out there. We couldn't do anything more. We told the police where he was but there's no arrest warrant for animal cruelty. We found his mother's house and we found out where he worked but there was no legal way of getting him back. The police said they couldn't [put an arrest warrant out], they said there was no power for animal cruelty.'

After the trial, Jan said Bobby had handed everything over to his children – including the animals – and she worried that they would continue in the business using his name. Moira denies that this is the case. Jan said: 'At the end of the trial they were talking about the fine. They said he had no money because actually during the trial he had signed everything over to his children so he had no money for them to take from him. That was my recollection of how that ended up. They carried on for a little while but through his children.'

Tim added: 'It does pass from the other to the other to the other and the name does go on down the generations. When we shut down Mary Chipperfield's circus, that moved to Spain although as a shadow of its former self. It was never the powerhouse that Mary Chipperfield's company was. Likewise, every now and again another member of the family pops up.'

CHAPTER 10

ISSUES

So Anne had settled into life at Longleat and all seemed to be going well, but the first signs of trouble were starting to emerge. It was originally agreed that it would only ever be a temporary place of safety to get her out of the circus, but as it became clear she would remain at the safari park, issues started to emerge between those interested in her welfare. ADI had agreed that she should go to Longleat initially, but ultimately wanted her to go to a sanctuary in the US. So from that point on, there were tensions between the group that helped save her from the circus and those now responsible for her welfare.

Tim Phillips of ADI says: 'She was arthritic and in a real state. It would probably have added a year to her life climate-wise.' His wife and colleague Jan Creamer adds that the US had good elephant sanctuaries where Anne could have been rehomed, including California-based PAWS (the Performing Animal Welfare Society) and the Elephant Sanctuary in Tennessee. But two vets who specialise in elephants – one working for the RSPCA, and the other working for SWS – concluded that she would not be able to travel overseas. ADI said at the time that she was used to transport and would have been OK, but the consensus from everyone else was that she would have to stay in Britain. Jon Cracknell at Longleat says that Anne has since been assessed by Susan Mikota from the Elephant Sanctuary in Tennessee, who has decided it is not viable to move her. There is the further issue that, although her health has improved, she is older and her arthritis will never be healed. In terms of other places in the UK that she can go, there are many issues with introducing her to existing herds of elephants in other zoos and safari parks.

So, with an overseas home ruled out, and not many options within the UK, the next step was how to improve her life at Longleat. In the aftermath of Anne's rescue, Jon Cracknell of Longleat had the idea of creating an elephant sanctuary at the safari park. There was a desperate need for a sanctuary in Europe to home ex-circus, zoo and safari park elephants, and Anne's arrival at the park was the perfect opportunity. He was planning to recruit other elephants from Europe to become her companions.

But it wasn't to be. After consultation with other sanctuaries, experts, charities and animal rights groups, it was decided that Longleat was not the ideal place for it. 'I was trying to push the idea of an elephant sanctuary because I didn't see us managing elephants for breeding and conservation,' Jon explains. 'At the time, I said that what we needed to focus on was that there were elephants that needed homes.' But when they did further research, they realised that Longleat didn't meet the criteria to become a sanctuary. The Global Federation of Animal Sanctuaries (GFAS) sets out a precise set of conditions that must be met. 'They have a strict but very good policy of what an animal sanctuary should be,' says Jon, 'and one of them is that you can't have paying people coming in. So we could never be an animal sanctuary but we could live with their ideals but also we're a commercial business... They were never going to make Anne do parades or dance for her supper, but we are a commercial business.'

A meeting had been held on Valentine's Day 2014 to decide how to proceed with the idea of a sanctuary. The attendance list is secret – Jon says that Longleat persuaded a number of animal welfare groups to attend who would never normally sit down with a zoo, which is what Longleat is classed as, so they remain anonymous. Those who did declare their attendance were Ed Stewart of PAWS which is a sanctuary based in California, plus Matt Ford of SWS, Deborah Bradfield

– an animal health inspector for the City of London – and Chris Draper of the Born Free Foundation. Having someone from PAWS attend was something of a coup as they run Ark 2000. Set in 2,300 acres in California, it is regarded as one of the best sanctuaries in the world. 'The idea was to critically appraise [the idea], look at what a sanctuary should be and look at what Longleat's options were,' says Jon.

The group ultimately decided that Longleat wasn't the right place for a sanctuary. Jon reflects: 'We saw the paper, we'd moved her in a week, within three days of the article we'd come up with this concept and actually in retrospect, was it the right thing to do? It was a sanctuary for Anne, great. She had nowhere else to go. But not for other elephants.' He adds: 'There was probably a naivety on my part. If I'd have been here a year, I probably wouldn't have been so effusive.'

So they decided to model Anne's Haven, her current home, on the ideals of a sanctuary. To meet these standards, they had to move to a model of 'protected contact', where there is no direct interaction with humans, as opposed to free contact. Protected contact is the accepted standard now for elephants in captivity in the Western world. With this concept, there is no need for bullhooks or chains, and the elephant can come and go as it pleases. The elephants are still trained as vets need access to them, but they are trained with food and word association rather than with bullhooks and chains and a trainer in the pen with them. 'Zoos are moving to protected contact,' says Jan Creamer from ADI, 'where no one goes into a space with an elephant with a weapon in their hand. That's the change in America, in Europe, that's the change everyone knows needs to be made.'

Anne had been free contact for her entire life and was therefore free contact for the first few years at Longleat. 'Free contact is about dominion,' says Jon Cracknell. 'You're part of the herd but you're the main character and you're dominating everything. It doesn't have to be physical violence. Some people do that but that's not really in this country. Protected contact is about elephants choosing to interact and if they don't want to, they'll just sod off. There's still an element of training but because they can walk away at any point it's not about dominion, it's about mutual respect.'

Although pretty much everyone was happy with the plans for the new elephant home, there was another complication: the issue of how long it took to get Anne there. The old elephant house had been converted for rhinos and wasn't a perfect home for her. Also, it was free contact, which meant using bullhooks on her. ADI, the Born Free Foundation, the RSPCA and even the Robertses started putting pressure on Longleat to stop the use of bullhooks and to move towards protected contact.

There were also issues with heating, flooring and access as Anne shared the old home, which was only ever supposed to be temporary, with a rhino. To replace it, *Daily Mail* readers and members of the public raised £410,000. But it took nearly four years for her new home to be constructed and for her to move in. Longleat blamed the long delay on the difficulties of obtaining planning permission as the safari park is built on Grade I parkland and Jon Cracknell mentions 'internal management wrangling' and funding issues. Whatever the reason, Longleat admits that this was a 'fail'. Anne was stuck in a sub-standard home for far longer than anticipated, which is particularly sad given she is in her twilight years. So although the plans for the new home were met with widespread approval, having been formulated with the help of leading elephant sanctuaries, the delays meant that groups including ADI, Born Free and the RSPCA became very frustrated with the situation. Jon says that the new elephant house was designed within six months of her arrival and the plan was to build within eight months, but he says there were a lot of 'challenges'. 'There was a lot of criticism – some of it rightly so,' he admits. 'We did take too long on it. It was always going to happen, it was just that there were funding issues, challenges of conservation heritage and internal challenges.'

Once the home was finally built and Anne moved in on 5 February 2015, yet another hurdle was to prove impossible to overcome: what to do about companionship. The experts are agreed that elephants should be kept together. They are highly sociable creatures, living in herds in the wild. There is an ongoing dispute between Longleat and those, including ADI, who say she should have the companionship of other elephants. They, and many others, think it is cruel to keep her on their own. But Anne's case is difficult: she has been reviewed by various experts and at the moment it doesn't seem sensible to send her anywhere else. Introducing new elephants to Longleat would mean that the safari park would have to maintain a herd and keep introducing new elephants so that none were left on their own – something no one wants. The Robertses have also insisted that Anne didn't like other elephants. Jon Cracknell said at the time that Anne's ears had previously been chewed from her interactions with other elephants. There is a worry that if she didn't get on with the new elephants, there would be a serious risk to her health. Longleat acknowledge that it is another 'fail' that she has no companion elephants.

When she was initially liberated, there was a suggestion that she could go to a zoo or safari park with existing herds but this was later decided against due to her health problems. Jon says there would have been serious issues of integrating her. 'It can work well or it can work terribly,' he explains. 'If you put her in with a healthy middle-aged cow or bull then there will be a dominance issue. If there is an argument, the risk with her ailment is that if she goes down, she may never get up. It's difficult because elephants should be in a group but if we're bringing in one, two, three new elephants, there will be a change in dynamics. If she hasn't got the capability to stand up to it and ultimately dies, we'll get criticism. And you can't step in. I saw an elephant kill another elephant recently [in the wild]. They're not benign creatures. It's like a moving train – you're not going to stop it. And even if you could, it takes two seconds and an animal's dead.'

Finding an elephant in a similar situation to Anne will always be hard, given she was Britain's last circus elephant. In the past Longleat has had other elephants in mind, but some of them have since died or continue to be embroiled in legal disputes and none appear likely to need a home in the near future. 'Now what that does mean is that ultimately Anne doesn't have companionship and it is a fail,' says Jon. 'I can't really justify it on the grounds that it's a good thing but it removes any risk of her being killed by another elephant. Ultimately, if Longleat felt it could provide for elephants long term, then great. It feels it can't, so we have to draw a line somewhere and that line is Anne. And Anne will be the last elephant at Longleat because Longleat doesn't have the facilities and environment suitable for keeping elephants in this country.'

One of the reasons why he is keen not to establish a herd at Longleat is because it might encourage more breeding in the UK or Europe, which will not benefit the species. 'The risk is if we take elephants from other collections, we're leaving an elephant-sized hole where they can bring in a younger one,' he explains. 'Actually, bringing in elephants doesn't benefit elephants as a whole – we could only bring three or four in with the space we've got and then that's the end of it as your focus is on them. We've then got that situation where when one dies, you bring another one in and so you're just perpetuating elephants here.'

So Longleat decided to change its focus and now invests £50,000 a year in helping elephants in the places where they are native. They help fund projects in Nepal and Sri Lanka and the idea is to improve welfare for captive or working elephants. 'The hope is that this will have a bigger impact than ploughing the money into one or two equally important animals,' says Jon. 'This way we utilise similar resources to have a greater impact and improve the lives of many elephants.'

Chris Draper from Born Free is in two minds about the outcome. He had wanted Anne to go to a sanctuary but he says: 'There was always that doubt: what if she's not healthy enough, what if she's not strong enough and ends up dying on the journey, worst case scenario, or actually having an injury, falling over and making things worse? I think all of us had that in the back of our minds that this might not be feasible, we just hoped it was. But the more that she was looked at by vets who knew what they were looking at, the more it was kind of clear that it's probably not going to happen.' He says that it is 'sad' because it would be a 'lovely end to her life' to live with other elephants in a sanctuary. 'It's not just that they've got more space,' he explains, 'they've also got the facilities to manage different groups of elephants at the same time so they can test out relationships without coming to harm.'

Ros Clubb from the RSPCA was also disappointed but realistic about Anne not being able to go to a sanctuary abroad. She says it was a 'really difficult decision' for everyone to make. 'There's that fear that she would be better off with other elephants but equally far worse if she gets moved into a group and they're not compatible. That could make her welfare much, much worse. There was always a question mark.' She believes Longleat's sanctuary idea to be the best option, though she would have preferred that it was not part of a safari park. 'Overall, everything weighed up, it's probably the best outcome,' she says. 'Ultimately, we would have loved to have gotten her over to the States to a sanctuary but it would have been too much risk for her, unfortunately.' She admits that she found Longleat's delays 'frustrating'.

ADI still think Anne should have access to other elephants, even if she is kept from directly interacting with them, possibly with barriers in between. Jan Creamer says: 'So they may get on and they like each other and if they don't, even if you can at least argue with a neighbour, that's still nice.' She also believes that Longleat were too willing to listen to Bobby's recommendations about Anne. 'It started very quickly, with Bobby Roberts saying: "Well, she doesn't like other elephants, so there's no point in introducing her to another elephant,"' she says. 'Well, he would say that, wouldn't he? That's his justification for keeping her alone.'

Jan believes it is crucial for elephants to have contact with other elephants. 'We've watched elephants at night contacting and conversing with each other when no other humans are around,' she says. 'We've watched elephants who, after one of them has been beaten, they reach out to each other. We saw it at Mary Chipperfield's. It was especially touching in the elephant barn at night how the three females would reach over to Rani [one of the beaten elephants] and touch her and also to the male. They would touch them in all the places where they had been hit and there was emotion in the way they communicated with each other. But Anne was never given the chance.'

She and Tim are also unimpressed with the choice of Anne's new companions, who are there instead of other elephants. 'She's got goats now,' says Tim, 'which is kind of like you being locked in a room with a chimp or a dog or a cat.'

ADI remain convinced that Anne should have been sent to a sanctuary abroad. 'Her life was transformed by the investigation and we're glad of that and it was important for her to be got out as quickly as possible given the kind of vagaries of British law,' Tim says. 'She did deserve better and there was a window, there was an opportunity to send her to the US. She was travelling on a regular basis just months before and we monitored that, we filmed it, so we knew how well she loaded, unloaded, and she was very used to travelling at that point.'

It's worth bearing in mind that for ADI, it was something of a slap in the face that Anne went to Longleat. Mary Chipperfield's father Jimmy founded it and she previously kept elephants there. One of Anne's keepers, Andy Hayton, had also previously looked after Mary Chipperfield's elephants. It is also worth bearing in mind that ADI are staunchly against animals in captivity and cannot be seen to compromise on this. At the time, they posted on their website the following statement: 'Many of our supporters will remember that many years ago, Longleat was run by the notorious Chipperfield family. However, they severed their ties with Longleat many years ago. This move does not indicate ADI's support of captive wildlife but we are taking a practical approach in that Anne needs to be somewhere with the facilities to care for her.'

But Jan and Tim concede that, although they don't believe that things are perfect for Anne, at least she has her freedom and she has a better life now. 'She was pulled out of hell and she went somewhere not great,' says Tim. 'She deserved better, but her life was transformed. She was out in the open air with the sun on her back – that's what I remember from when I first saw her at Longleat.' He says that it was a 'shame' the luxury elephant house wasn't built more quickly, which would have given her 'four years of absolute bliss'. He adds: 'She really deserved that. She'd had such a horrible, horrible life that those twilight years could've been as good as possible. I think that's what everyone wanted for her – the fairytale ending instead of a compromise – but you reach a point where you know that in terms of our influence, this is as good as it's going to get for Anne and it's a shame and she deserved better, but at least she got the sun on her back and a better diet.'

'She's definitely in a better place than she had been so she is away from the abuse and out in the open air,' Jan concludes.

CHAPTER 11

CRUELTY IN CIRCUSES

Shackled to the floor with iron chains and beaten by her groom, there can be little debate that Anne suffered during her time in the circus. But are circuses inherently cruel to animals? Are some animals more suited to circus life than others? Dogs and horses are easy to train and these training methods are not generally thought to be cruel. Parrots seem to enjoy mimicking human speech and some animals, like cats, clearly enjoy human company and are happy to be around humans without having to be held captive. But elephants, lions, tigers and bears seem to be in another category. These wild animals are not natural companions of humans and are dangerous to them. Training does not come naturally to them, though they are clever, and it's hard to believe that they enjoy what they are trained to do in the circus ring in the same way as dogs and parrots seem to. Also, Britain is not the natural habitat for any of these wild animals and sometimes they develop health problems as a result. Anne's leg problems cannot have been helped by cold, wet English winters.

There is plenty of literature on the subject. A report on elephants in captivity led by the RSPCA in 2008 found that they lived short, stressed lives, blighted by disease and injury. Asian elephants in European zoos and safari parks survived just nineteen years on average, half the lifespan of those working in Burmese timber camps. Also, stillbirth and infant deaths were higher among the captive population, according to the piece in the journal *Science*. The scientists scrutinised data on the welfare of more than 4,500 female elephants. Almost 800 were kept in European zoos between 1960 and 2005. The rest lived either in Kenya or Burma. Many of the animals were obese due to a high-calorie diet and a lack of exercise and so struggled with pregnancy and labour. The authors called for a ban on importing elephants as a result.

A 1997 report by the All-Party Parliamentary Group for Animal Welfare found disturbing signs of insanity in many circus animals. The report stated that the animals frantically chewed the bars of their cages for hours on end. They were confined to cages so small that they could move only one or two steps in any direction and were inevitably driven insane through frustration and boredom. It also found that lions and tigers in circuses can spend more than three-quarters of their time in box-like travelling cages on the backs of lorries.

The experts agree that elephants aren't suitable for life in circuses. Professor Stephen Harris, a mammal expert at the University of Bristol, says that the nature of circuses and zoos meant elephants were often kept alone, which he described as 'solitary confinement' for them. 'One of the points we made in our review of the welfare of elephants in captivity is that they have large spatial requirements and they have large mobility requirements which can't be met in zoos, let alone circuses,' he explains. 'Also, they have very specific social structures which are lifelong and quite complex and they're built on kin and of course keeping an elephant by itself is contrary to everything we know about these animals.' He says Anne's life at the circus would have been 'utterly grim, I might say appalling. It's like living in solitary confinement because you've got no one to interact with. Elephants are sociable, they're not solitary. They live extremely complex social lives and to deprive them of that before you do anything else, to me, is cruelty.' He adds that the outcome of her living on her own at Longleat was 'far from ideal'.

As for wild animals in circuses, Professor Harris is scathing. 'We can't meet their basic welfare requirements and I don't see why on earth we want animals performing tricks. It's a dominance thing. It always made me smile when I went round British zoos and the elephant keepers who have this macho thing to them would be there in mid-winter wearing their shorts and T-shirts like they were on safari. It's the whole machismo thing: "Look at me, how good I am. I've got dominance over a big animal." To me, it's exactly the same as the horrors we've seen in the press recently about trophy shooting. People like to pose next to pictures with giraffes they've shot or a lion: "Look at me, how wonderful I am, I've just managed to kill a big animal." It's exactly the same: "Look at me, I haven't killed a big animal but I've got it wrapped round my little finger." I find it very offensive. I find the whole imagery of posing with animals to show how great you are offensive in whatever form it takes.'

Jon Cracknell of Longleat says he has mixed feelings about circuses. Asked whether he thought it was right to have elephants in circuses, he declares: 'Shouldn't happen. Full stop.' But other animals? 'Morally and ethically no, but do some of them enjoy it?' he says. 'It's difficult. I think some of the dogs and that probably really enjoy the attention and enjoy the training. If you look at Crufts, they're running through the hoops and tents so what's the difference between that and doing it in a Big Top?' He highlights the case of rescue parrots at Longleat, who were all previously abused and plucked their own feathers at one point as a result. They put on a show at Longleat but they have ten parrots and only three can perform at once. The parrots who are left out go 'mental' because they want to be involved, he says. 'So if you're asking if I would support the banning of wild animals in circuses, I already have. I've signed the petitions,' he adds. 'I think with zoos there's an element of conservation and education and you lose that in circuses. But saying that, I think it's easy to ban elephants and wild animals definitely shouldn't be in circuses, but when it comes down to some of the dogs and cats and horses… If it's done well, and their welfare's maintained and consideration is given to what you're trying to do and achieve, and consideration is given to the individual animals, then I can't say that it shouldn't happen but it doesn't feel right.'

Anne's osteopath Tony Nevin thinks that circuses are not good for the health of elephants: 'We now know it's not a good idea to get elephants balancing on balls or doing handstands or stuff like that. It's also not good for them to stand up for protracted periods on their hind legs. So while they will choose to do that in the wild when they're browsing or trying to climb something or pull something down, they're probably not doing it to the same degree in the circus when they're performing. It's like a repetitive strain injury for them.' He adds: 'I'm not really keen on elephants in circuses. I think there's a place for them in captivity as long as they're looked after properly and given everything that they need to be elephants. In an ideal world it'd be great if they were all in the wild, but if they were, poaching would decimate most of them as it is with most species, so there's a role for captive ones not just as ambassadors but also as DNA gene pools.'

Khyne U Mar, a University of Sheffield professor and trained vet, has studied elephants across Asia and says that the process of extracting them from the wild for a life in the circus or in captivity is inevitably cruel. Her study of more than 5,000 elephants explored the differences between those born in captivity and those caught in the wild, like Anne almost certainly was. The main problem with capturing elephants from the wild was 'chronic stress', she says. She wrote: 'Most elephants are captured at a relatively young age, causing their social structure to collapse with the loss of their mentors at a time when their independent foraging skills are still insufficient to meet their requirements.'

In her PhD, she also explored the ongoing stresses of being broken. 'The taming or breaking procedure undoubtedly incorporates stress and compromises the welfare of the animal, especially during the first few days of taming,' she wrote. 'Freshly caught elephants and those four- to five-year-old calves born in captivity are first put into crushes. The trainers use food and water wisely as a reward during the breaking operation. Until thoroughly obedient, which usually takes place after about three days, the calf does not see any other elephants. Later on, trained elephants are brought alongside the crush and fed and handled in full view of the captive. As soon as it has learned to be obedient, the trainee is taken out of the crush, but held loosely through the breast band (cradle) or tied to a tree. Thereafter its progress is rapid.' She says that the term 'breaking' is used to bring about the elephant's 'total submission to the will of humans'. The elephant usually refused food and water for the first few days, but after this 'its spirit is more or less broken and it starts to accept food and water'.

Animal charities and pressure groups all believe circuses are incompatible with high standards of animal welfare. Indeed, the UK's premier animal welfare group, the RSPCA, says that the travelling circus life is likely to have a harmful effect on animals. 'The complex needs of wild animals can never be adequately met in a circus environment,' it says. 'Regular transport, cramped and bare temporary housing, forced training and performance are all unavoidable realities for the animals. Tigers and lions, who'd typically roam for miles every day in the wild, spend the majority of their lives in a space tens of thousands of times smaller than their natural roaming range on beastwagons and in makeshift runs. Some animals are simply tethered to a peg in the ground, unable to move beyond a few metres. It's not uncommon to see circus animals displaying repetitive behaviours such as pacing and rocking from side to side. They're not dancing: these can be signs of stress, of suffering from poor welfare.' Dr Ros Clubb, senior wildlife scientist for the RSPCA and their elephant specialist, says: 'Conditions such as confinement to beastwagons and cramped temporary cages, transporting them from site to site and exposing them to abnormal social groups and noisy conditions all add up to a recipe for poor animal welfare.'

Dr Clubb adds that elephants shouldn't be in circuses. 'The main thing is the travelling aspect and the performance,' she says. 'So transport is known to be stressful in confining the animal but also because you have to travel you can't build a nice big enclosure with pools and mud baths and scratching posts and complex environments and all the things that you would expect from keeping an elephant in captivity. So effectively they get a ring-fenced bit of field if they're lucky but you don't know what the site's like. So it might be a car park, it might be a field, it might have access to water, it might be waterlogged... There's no consistency.' She adds: 'We have concerns with not just how the animals are handled now but how they were trained in the past to respond to commands and using the ankus to train them. The principles behind this are of negative reinforcement, of punishment – we've moved on from that. It's widely recognised that they are not good for animal welfare.' She says the major problems with elephants in circuses are the 'transient' nature of the temporary enclosures they are provided with, the fact that they're chained up a lot of the time, together with the repetitive nature of the performance, which she says has been linked to a host of welfare problems including joint problems and hernias.

ADI was set up specifically to target circuses with performing animals and they claim to have infiltrated more than twenty over the years. As a result, they have a lot of first-hand knowledge of life in circuses. It is often said of Anne that she can't have suffered greatly because she is Europe's oldest elephant and is still going strong. At one point, her former keeper at Longleat even congratulated Bobby on having done a good job. But ADI give this view short shrift: 'What we always find is that most animals in circuses die young,' Tim Phillips explains. 'They've got a hell of a rate of chewing through animals but against the odds you get these grand old survivors. Anne is astonishing. I think the fact is that everyone else died and that's why it's so galling when they say: "Oh, she must've been treated well because she lived to this grand old age". It's as idiotic as saying someone can't have been treated badly during the Holocaust because there are survivors that make it to 100. There are some incredibly resilient people and animals. And I remember people were saying she may have to be put down and Jan [Creamer] pointed out that she has been chained to the ground, unable to move for four months. She's a survivor.'

ADI, like many others, believes it is not just the violence that makes circuses cruel, but the miserable day-to-day existence the animals lead. 'We believe the confinement, the deprivation, the social isolation is, if anything, worse than the violence they endure,' says Tim. 'Anne was saved from the circus because she was beaten but she survived incredible hardship. I could not live through what she went through without going out of my mind. It's the equivalent of being kidnapped, not knowing what the hell's going on, being hooded and finding yourself handcuffed to a radiator in Iran and just never knowing if you're going to be free, never seeing anyone and having your food shoved under a door. That's what breaks people much more than physical torture, that kind of isolation and deprivation. And that's why to us it was so important to give her that glimpse of companionship, to see another elephant on the horizon, to hear another trumpet.'

It appears to be undeniable that circuses don't seem like happy places for animals. There have been a number of high-profile cases in recent years of keepers being appallingly violent to their animals. I asked ADI whether they thought violence was endemic to circuses. They have run undercover investigations into Mary Chipperfield's Circus, the Great British Circus, Have Trunk Will Travel in California and then of course Bobby – and in each case found elephants being mistreated. 'This violence to elephants is consistent,' says Tim. 'It's not just a few bad apples – it's everywhere we go.'

Jan Creamer agrees that there is a link between circuses and violence: 'They're afraid of the animals. They've got them in a place where they shouldn't have them, up close to them.' Recalling one of the worst cases of violence at a circus, she says Steve Gills, an elephant keeper at Mary Chipperfield's company, managed to bend a bullhook on the back of an elephant because he hit it so hard. Tim Phillips says of that investigation: 'It was so savage, the violence, because they were completely unguarded. And we said: "OK, we will only put into evidence hits over the head with a weapon and multiple blows," so if you hit the elephant in the face once it didn't go in and we still put in more than 300 incidents. There's one where he [Gills] hits an elephant in the face – turns the broom upside down and hits it thirty-two times in the face, just again and again and again. Absolute headcase! He was urinating on the elephants and beating them.'

Jan says: 'He'd be changing the water or whatever, leave them and go out of the barn and then almost stop and come back in and start hitting them for no reason. It was so psychotic. You think, why? What's the reason for this?'

And it wasn't just Gills who was being violent to the animals. His boss, Mary Chipperfield, was prosecuted for beating a baby chimp. She was one of the foremost animal trainers in the country when ADI began to infiltrate her business, and was supplying animals for everything from television adverts and parties to Disney films, including the animals for *101 Dalmatians*. Tim says the Chipperfield investigation was particularly disturbing. He recalls that when they started watching the tapes, they gradually realised how much abuse was going on: 'We thought, Jesus, this is a stunning level of violence starting to emerge!'

Jan adds: 'It seemed insane. It was a barrage of violence. Everywhere you looked, an animal was being punched. It was like hell! The thing that I always remember from her trial was when they showed the video of her beating the baby chimpanzee and the prosecutor said to her: "When you see the video of yourself, what do you think, what do you feel about yourself when you see yourself on screen like that? Any regrets?" and she said: "No, I don't think anything at all. There's no difference between the way I treat my animals and the way I raise my children." There was actually a collective gasp – the whole court was like: "Did she really say that?" Stunning!'

Tim says the ADI investigation into the industry made the public aware of the nature of violence towards animals in circuses. The group called their investigation 'The Ugliest Show on Earth' and it involved infiltrating thirteen circuses around the world with a number of investigators recording evidence. Tim recalls: 'A huge body of evidence in one go came out. The thing we found was an utterly casual regard for violence – it wasn't just like it was isolated incidents where something would happen and it would escalate and someone would be angry or frustrated with the animal because it wouldn't go in or something, it was just casual brutality. If you look at the case of the Great British Circus, when someone wanders past – say, if someone's hitting an elephant in the tent and this person's on their own – they'll make no attempt to conceal their actions. One of the things we noticed in the Mary Chipperfield case – we had cameras all over the place by the end of it – was that they were all picking up this violence, so you'd have Mary Chipperfield talking to someone from outside the elephant barn and inside was this obvious beating going on. It was just normal.'

Tim says that there seemed to him to be the same approach at Bobby Roberts' circus. 'We got a stunning amount of violence in that barn,' he says. 'But there's no looking over the shoulder and sometimes there are several other people in the barn who are workers.' Jan adds: 'When a normal person is looking at that and sees video after video, it strikes you how casual it is and it's apparent that nobody thinks anything of it.' Tim continues: 'Those are not the actions of people who think they will be in trouble for kicking, hitting, spitting on those animals. I think the spitting in the camel's face shows the utter contempt.'

Chris Draper of the Born Free Foundation says that most elephants in circuses suffered violence during their training. 'I think most trained elephants have been subjected to a period of their life where they've had the, for want of a better phrase, crap beaten out of them and it's from that that all this stems,' he explains. 'Once you subject them to that, they know every end of the sharp stick and everywhere that that sharp stick will get them. You don't need to do much with a bullhook ever again because they know exactly what it means. So I'm not saying each time they touch it [the elephant]with a bullhook that they are inflicting pain but they are using an implement which was used to inflict pain previously, otherwise the elephant wouldn't know why to move its leg or move its bum, whatever it is.' He adds: 'The other thing with circuses is [that] it's not just about what goes on in the ring or how the elephants are trained, it's about the life on the road. Even if the animals loved the ring, which I don't believe they do, I bet they don't love living in the trailer. I bet they don't love spending most of the months of the year on the road. I think that's almost more important to me in terms of meeting their natural behaviour requirements.'

Bobby Roberts was found guilty of allowing Anne to suffer while in the care of Nicolae Nitu. He was also criticised for not giving his staff proper training. This is another issue for circuses: the employment of cheap, unskilled workers with no background in animal keeping. It was one of the reasons ADI found it so easy to infiltrate multiple circuses and expose cruelty to the animals. 'This is common with people in circuses,' says Tim. 'They just take on people with no skills whatsoever. I worked undercover during the Chipperfield investigation and I told them I was a painter and decorator and could I have a job for a while and got it. We just sailed in. That's the sort of background you have if you're looking after the animals in those places.' Using unskilled, untrained, cheap labour means that circuses don't have huge outgoings but it also means that they have workers with no training or skills caring for animals with complex welfare needs. This means that when the trained animals do not respond correctly as the workers cannot handle them, the workers get increasingly annoyed and resort to violence. This can be seen in the video from Bobby Roberts' circus.

Khyne U Mar says that the lack of training and understanding of an elephant often leads to violent behaviour. Describing what she thought when she saw the video of Anne being abused, she says: 'The person simply does not understand how to deal with her.' She says that Anne did not understand what the keeper wanted her to do because he was untrained – 'Anne is confused so there is a time lapse. This time lapse makes the keeper feel like she's not following what he wants her to do and that's when he starts abusing because he simply does not understand animal behaviour.'

Jon Cracknell of Longleat also agrees that the violence stems from a problem of communication. He referred to footage ADI previously took of Anne with previous keepers at the circus. A video shows them trying to move her from an outside area to her barn. She refuses and so they produce a pair of pliers and attempt to drag her by the ear. At first she resists but then, clearly in pain, she relents. Referring to this, he says: 'I think Bobby knew how to work elephants but no one else did, so they just did what they could and Anne is stubborn and if she doesn't want to go somewhere, she ain't going anywhere. I think if you're inexperienced, you could get frustrated and they did leather her a bit. But if I saw something like that happening on my park, I would fire them on the spot.'

Nor are other experts in the field surprised at the seemingly universal cruelty to elephants in captivity. Professor Stephen Harris, who gave evidence to a Defra Circus Working Group, told the *Daily Mail* in 2011: 'What has happened to Anne is disgusting, but not unexpected. You can't control big wild animals without the use of force, and that means regularly beating the living daylights out of them. It's as simple as that. For this reason, and for many others, wild animals should not be allowed in circuses.'

In 2008, Professor Harris was commissioned to write a report on the welfare of elephants in zoos in Britain. Defra and the RSPCA among others commissioned the study to fill a research gap. Perhaps the best summary of its findings was one of its conclusions: 'There was not a single elephant in the UK that did not have a welfare concern in the opinion of one or two of the researchers.' It also found that 75 per cent of the elephants in zoos at the time were classed as being overweight. What's more worrying still is that zoos are regarded as having higher welfare standards than circuses.

Professor Harris also says that violence to elephants in circuses is inevitable. 'We have this concept that elephants should be trained and taught to do tricks and do what we want, and the only way you do that is frankly by dominating them and that does include violence.' He adds that the process of training an elephant by breaking was extremely violent. 'It's based on a mixture of starvation, chaining, beating and breaking and also once they're broken, just maintaining it. I can remember being on an Asian elephant in Corbett National Park in India and riding a female, who was misbehaving. The mahouts were all carrying ankuses, which is essentially a lump of metal, a metal bar. This female was misbehaving and he beat her on the head with it, and she still carried on and he beat her senseless, and in the end she collapsed to the ground and the howdah [platform] we were on just fell sideways. That's how they maintain it.'

Asked about the general principles of training elephants, Professor Harris says that it is by subjugating them. 'You can try positive reinforcement in non-contact systems but to get them to do tricks, a lot of it is by basic subjugation which involves some level of violence or brutality or withholding something until they do what you want. All the things you want them to do are based on them knowing who the boss is and you have to have a very high level of control over an elephant to be happy to have it stand there with members of the public. That elephant has to know that if it misbehaves, it's in trouble. I don't see how else you do it. People argue that it's positive reinforcement all the way – well, that's not what you see in Asia, it's not what you see in elephant books when they describe how they train those elephants. I have trouble believing people who say they do it through positive reinforcement. The fact that there's so much evidence of Anne being brutalised [referring to ADI footage and previous footage of workers dragging her by her ear with pliers] shows that plays a role in showing who's the boss.'

Simon Adams, an independent zoo and veterinary advisor who has assessed Anne for both Bobby and ADI, agrees that violence is necessary to train an elephant for a circus: 'Elephants are huge and it is usually very much whoever's the biggest is the boss so you have to dominate the elephant physically so that you're seen as the leader and then they'll follow what you do. The biggest problem is that if you're going to be training elephants for circuses, you can't be physically bigger than them but you can control their movements, control their feeding and control their pain. So unfortunately, especially as an elephant grows, they will continually challenge for leader, so if you're working with elephants you have to recognise when they're challenging and beat them. This is why they're inappropriate to be used for training. In my view it is cruel to train them because you could use as many rewards as you like, but ultimately they are going to challenge you and you have to inflict pain on them to control them. You've seen from all the exposé videos that ADI and others have done that a lot of the guys who are working closely with them are being cruel because they've been trained to be – because it's a necessity that you do not let the elephant become dominant to you, because as soon as it does you can't work with that animal anymore because it won't accept you leading it.' He says, simply: 'Violence is necessary to train an elephant. There is no other way.' He adds that he thought that the ADI footage showed 'normal circus elephant management and training' and concludes: 'Which is why you shouldn't have them being trained for the circus.'

There are numerous other examples of keepers mistreating elephants and other circus animals. In 2006, three zoo workers at Twycross Zoo in Leicestershire were arrested on suspicion of causing unnecessary suffering to an animal after two elephants were allegedly beaten. At the time, a spokesman for the zoo said that one of the elephants was a twenty-eight-year-old female Asian called Tonzi and the other a sixteen-year-old called Noorjahan.

The zoo said the elephants had not suffered any lasting ill effects. The three members of staff were dismissed and the zoo reported the incident to the police. The zoo said that the mistreatment involved 'rogue individuals' who acted 'in complete disregard to their moral, contractual and legal requirements'. Police passed files on two members of staff to the CPS, who decided not to take further action based on a lack of evidence.

The general unhappiness of elephants in circuses can also be seen in how often they escape and attack their keepers. In St Louis, Missouri, in 2014, three elephants escaped from the Moolah Shrine Circus and ran amok, damaging cars before being recaptured by members of staff. In Ireland, in 2012, a three-tonne Indian elephant bolted through Cork city centre after fleeing Courtney's Circus. And in 2008, an elephant was killed in a road collision in Mexico after it escaped the Circo Union circus.

But those who live and work in circuses insist that the animals are well-treated and not generally abused. Martin Lacey, director of The Great British Circus, told the *Daily Mail* in 2006: 'The idea that circuses are cruel is the biggest myth since the tooth fairy. In 150 years the RSPCA has managed to get only five convictions against circuses. We're treated worse than lepers and gypsies.' Chris Barltrop, a spokesman for the European Circus Association, which also represents the interests of the UK industry, told the *Mail* that circuses treat their animals with kindness and compassion. 'I've worked in circuses for over thirty years and I've never seen any deliberate cruelty,' he insisted. 'The animals are well looked after and look forward to performing. Animals will only work for you if there's mutual love and understanding. The trainers work in partnership with their animals. They stroke and pat their lions and tigers. They will even tickle their stomachs.'

Perhaps the most interesting defender of wild animals in circuses is Thomas Chipperfield. With more than 300 years of animal training in his blood, Britain's last big cat trainer has continued to tour the country with a big cat act comprising of three tigers and two lions. He is from a true circus family with a lineage even more impressive than Bobby Roberts'. His ancestor James Chipperfield introduced performing exotic animals to Britain, exhibiting his menagerie on the frozen Thames in London at the Frost Fair of 1684. In the 1950s, Chipperfield's Circus was the biggest in Europe, with a tent that seated 6,000, a herd of sixteen elephants and more than 200 other animals, including polar bears and chimps. Thomas's great-uncle Jimmy Chipperfield created the safari parks at Longleat, Woburn, Knowsley and other locations. In 2015, Jolly's circus announced that it was dropping the big cat act; they didn't say why. But Thomas continues with the performance – billed as 'An Evening with Lions and Tigers' – which last took place at Welshpool, Powys, in July 2015. Before that, the animals were last seen at the winter quarters on a cold hillside in Scotland – a very different climate to the one they are used to. There were suggestions from animal protection groups that the big cats are confined to beastwagons and have limited access to an exercise pen but Peter Jolly's Circus denied this.

During July 2015, Thomas toured Wales with two three-year-old lions called Tsavo and Assegai, a seventeen-year-old female tiger called Nadia and two young tigers called Syas and Altai. According to a feature article in the *Daily Telegraph*, he had performed with Peter Jolly's Circus in 2014 in an act in which the lions leapt over his shoulders from one podium to the next and roared for the crowds before kissing their trainer at the end. Giving a fascinating insight into the world of a big cat tamer, Thomas Chipperfield, twenty-four at the time, said there was a complex relationship between animal and trainer. He told the newspaper: 'They have to perceive you as the alpha male, but you have to be the boss in a way that doesn't force them to resent you or be afraid of you. It's a fine line to walk, because if you're too soft, you're perceived as weak, and if you're too hard, you're seen as a threat, and either way you're going to get hurt. You can't afford to mistreat a lion or tiger, because eventually they will turn. They will realise they are a lot stronger, faster and more dangerous than you, and it can only end very badly.'

Many big cat tamers have learned this lesson the hard

way. Thomas's second cousin Richard Chipperfield suffered brain injury and partial paralysis after being bitten in the head by a tiger while working for the Ringling Brothers and Barnum & Bailey Circus in Florida in 1998. In 2013, a trainer was killed by a tiger during a show in Mexico, another was mauled during a performance in Spain.

Performing animals in circuses have long been a primary target of animal rights protesters, including the animals of Thomas's second cousin Mary Chipperfield. But Thomas points out that there have been only a handful of prosecutions of circus trainers in the past 130 years – 'I doubt if that's one per cent of the trainers in Britain in that time' – and asks people not to judge his profession by the actions of individuals. But the reality is that it tends to take an animal campaign group to break into the site to film what really happens behind closed doors. And animal rights groups are scathing – particularly of Thomas's act, which they see as a step backwards in terms of a ban on wild animals in circuses. Dr Ros Clubb of the RSPCA says: 'Chipperfield's is attempting a kind of rebranding: "Come and see our educational show, we're going to tell you about the conservation of tigers," which is just laughable. It's just another circus.'

WAS BOBBY [illegible] TO [illegible]

[illegible]

CHAPTER 12

WAS BOBBY CRUEL TO HER?

It's one thing to decide that circuses are cruel and that violence seems to occur with depressing regularity to the elephants kept in them, but whether or not Bobby Roberts was cruel to Anne is a whole other matter. There are mixed feelings and it is an emotional subject, hugely polarised. But opinions about him are inevitably based on feelings towards animals in captivity in general. So for ADI and others, Bobby mistreated Anne. But for those who work in the captive animals industry and have come into contact with him, he is a misunderstood relic of a past era who had the best intentions.

Those who are now involved in Anne's care seem to be of the belief that Bobby simply hasn't changed while the world around him has altered dramatically. Where once the public was delighted and amazed by wild animals in circuses, there are few who would appreciate them now. And animal welfare standards have influenced and been influenced by this change in attitude. But Bobby was left behind, unaware or unable to appreciate why his methods were now no longer acceptable. Those who are now responsible for Anne's care are almost all agreed that although the situation that she was kept in wasn't ideal, Bobby did have genuine affection for Anne and the other animals he owned.

Jon Cracknell's views on the subject are typical of this standpoint: 'I'm not saying what he did was right but I think he's of a different era and the world's changed around him and people are more aware. I just think he lives in a bubble but I don't think he's malicious. I think he loved Anne and I think he still does. I think he loves all his animals, he just sees them in a different way. That's not to say what he does is right or the use of animals in such performances is right but it is a case of saying I think you have to look at the context.' He added: 'I've seen people abusing animals and they do it because they're malicious and evil people. I've seen that around the world, I've seen it in the UK and I wouldn't put him in that camp.'

However, he's less complimentary about the way she was kept. 'I didn't feel the Robertses were bad people or malicious, but at the same time I didn't feel the barn..,' he tails off. 'There wasn't an opportunity for her to go in and out – she didn't have access to much outside. There was a field she could be taken down to, but I don't know how often that was happening. So the reality was if I saw that set-up as a zoo inspector, I wouldn't say it was acceptable long term. It depends how long she was in there for. She might be able to walk out of her paddock every day – I don't know what the management system was so I can't comment – but the fact she wasn't able to walk far, and I think she spent more time in there than out, I would say isn't great.' Jon says that when he went to see her home, he found a big barn with a big straw bed. 'Now the video shows something very different over three weeks, where she's chained continually on a pallet,' he says. When asked about her medical treatment at the circus and Bobby's insistence that she wouldn't take the painkillers, he simply says: 'We don't have trouble giving her treatment, put it that way.'

Ryan Hockley, one of Anne's original keepers and now head of safari at Longleat, agrees with Jon's assessment of the Robertses. When asked if Bobby was a relic from a previous age, he says: 'Yes, he is, but I don't mean that as a criticism but an observation. He's a dying breed. Wild animals in circuses in the UK is a done thing, and I'm sure it'll be the same across Europe soon, but particularly elephants in circuses. You're not going to see those for much longer.' He adds that he thought Anne and Bobby had a bond. 'I truly believe he and Anne had a good relationship,' he insists. 'How that relationship was formed, I don't know, but the end result seemed to be that they were comfortable with each other and he did actually care for her. That went for Anne too. She knew Bobby and he cared for her.'

Nic Masters, Anne's vet when she arrived at Longleat, thinks that although her care wasn't ideal when she was with the Robertses, they weren't to blame. When I ask him what he thinks, he says: 'I'm going to sound like a politician here. I think they didn't look after her in the way we would look after her in a good modern zoo. I think they probably looked after her in a way that they certainly wouldn't have thought of as cruel themselves, and was accepted practice in theirs and other circuses in days gone by. So I would have been very uncomfortable if she was still at the circus, being looked after in the way that she was, but I'm also uncomfortable being highly critical of them because I don't think they thought they were doing anything wrong, really.' He adds that her winter quarters were 'limited' and she didn't have much 'stimulation'.

Anne's osteopath Tony Nevin thinks Bobby did well by Anne when she was younger but he thinks that as Bobby got older and employed other people to look after her, 'that's when the problems set in. They [the Robertses] certainly looked after her, you couldn't really complain from that point of view. They treated her like a giant family pet,' he says. 'Bobby's heart was in the right place. You either like circuses or hate them but he was from a completely different time when childcare, teaching, everything in this country was different and I do feel he's sort of been targeted a little bit unfairly. He's not a highly-educated person, he's got a lot of practical experience and knowledge, but his physical health was failing him and he employed the wrong person to look after her. That's his crime, if that's what you want to call it.'

RSPCA inspector Jody Gordon echoes this sentiment. 'Bobby was brought up in the circus and the way they treated their animals was perfectly acceptable thirty years ago, they just didn't move with the times. He genuinely believed he was doing the right thing for his animals because that's the way he'd been brought up. I think he understood certainly by the end that he could have done more but he was stuck in a rut and I think he genuinely believed he wasn't doing a great deal wrong and that people were out to get circuses. I certainly never believed Bobby was cruel.'

Animal rights groups clearly disagree. ADI's views on Bobby have already been set out at length, as have those of the Born Free Foundation. But the RSPCA's standpoint is less clear-cut. They campaign for a ban on wild animals in circuses and yet they inspected Anne several times over the years and could find no evidence that Bobby was being cruel despite his later conviction for causing her unnecessary suffering. At times, they even praised elements of his care. They were criticised in the wake of the story for not noticing her condition before. ADI are particularly critical of the RSPCA for not doing more to help free Anne from her situation sooner so that she might have a chance of going to a sanctuary in the US. They questioned why her health issues and her inadequate medical treatment weren't picked up during routine inspections by both the RSPCA and for a Defra consultation on wild animals in circuses. 'We researched the Polebrook inspections of Anne,' says Jan, 'and she had been inspected in the barn a couple of times and nothing had been noticed.' She adds that an RSPCA inspector had submitted reports to court but they hadn't identified any issues. 'For us, what was significant was you had an elephant owned by a circus, in a barn, so she was in her winter quarters. It was being inspected and nobody noticed that there was something wrong. Nobody noticed that she was chained.'

At times, the authorities even seemed to praise the Robertses' care. In 2007, Chris Barltrop, chairman of Defra's committee on circus animals, said they were confident Anne was in the best possible place with Bobby. 'Independent veterinary advice we have seen suggests that her welfare needs are best met by her remaining with the circus,' he said. 'Allowing Anne into the circus ring to have her photograph taken will in no way affect her overall welfare. Indeed her welfare is possibly enhanced by the human contact and activity.' The following year, RSPCA inspector Jody Gordon visited the Robertses' circus in Huntingdon and said: 'The animals are in good health but there are concerns, particularly about how the elephant is kept. She is chained up for a lot of the time in a cage. But the stabling conditions are generally very good and they are kept in good health.'

But despite the concerns of other animal welfare groups, the RSPCA say they simply weren't ever able to find evidence that Bobby had committed a crime until the footage emerged. Jody Gordon says that for many years, RSPCA inspectors didn't have the knowledge or training to assess the welfare of exotic animals. 'Our inspectors have been visiting Bobby Roberts' circus for many years. Unfortunately, not many of our inspectors, if any at all, are really trained in recognising the welfare signs in elephants so you'd get reports coming back from inspectors saying: "Went to the circus, saw an elephant, looked in good bodily condition. No problems."' He says that this approach reinforced Bobby's conviction that he was in the right. 'There was a genuine belief that he wasn't doing anything wrong and that was the way it should be done and of course he never got in trouble. He was never investigated. He would have the inspectors visiting and telling him things were ok and telling him there was no investigation against him because there wasn't.'

Another major problem was the law. The only

really relevant legislation at the time was the Animal Welfare Act which required those caring for animals to meet good practice. But the reality is that no one had established what good practice was in a circus. And Dr Ros Clubb of the RSPCA tells me their lawyers were never sure they had enough for a prosecution until the footage emerged. She says: 'No one's established what good practice is in the circus. There was a real question mark over what is an offence in a circus environment. Legally there was doubt at our end as to whether [a prosecution] would be successful. But when it came to beating [in the footage], that was quite straightforward.'

Despite this, the RSPCA and Born Free had discussions with the Robertses about retiring her and by 2009 the Robertses themselves say they were keen for her to go to a new home. Ros says she and Jody met with Bobby around 2009 to ask him to give her up. 'We were really concerned about her welfare and we wanted for her to be moved out of the circus environment especially because we knew she had some kind of problem with her joints,' she says. 'We had a chat with Bobby, who genuinely seemed to want to do the best for her, and we talked about what if a suitable home was found for her, probably in this country because he really didn't think she'd be able to make a trip overseas. The only two elephant sanctuaries are in the States and there was concern with her age and her health whether she would survive a journey like that.' She says he was 'open' to the possibility but, sadly, there were no good options available. 'We went away trying to find a place for her and we couldn't find anywhere. It was a difficult situation.' Integrating her into an existing herd could be problematic given Bobby's assertion that she didn't like other elephants, the possibility she might have had disease and her arthritis problems. Longleat wasn't on the radar because it was a decade since they'd had elephants.

Jody Gordon recalls Bobby saying he would allow Anne to retire. 'Bobby told us he wanted her to go to a new home and not be travelling with him anymore which we promptly went away to do. But there was nowhere suitable. Nobody was prepared to take on an elephant of her age or introduce her to a herd. We weren't convinced even then that she was healthy enough to go to a sanctuary in America.' In any case, it was to take another two years before she was eventually rehomed, by which time she was into her seventh decade.

For everyone involved, the greatest mystery was that the Robertses still wanted to keep Anne despite the poor publicity she attracted and the reputation of cruelty that she gave the circus. She could do little more than pose for photographs in the ring for £6 a time, which, while it probably made a bit of money, certainly didn't cover the cost of keeping her. The Robertses themselves say this didn't remotely cover her upkeep. So why did they not give her up earlier? Looking back through newspaper cuttings over the years, it seems the couple always responded to this entreaty in the same way. This is a typical response from Bobby in 2005 to the *Daily Mail*: 'Even if I was offered £1 million, I wouldn't give Anne away. I love Anne. She's one of our family. She's like one of the children. If Anne went anywhere else, she'd miss me. She'd pine for me and die. She only reacts to me. She's lived with us for nearly fifty years. Anne wants to be here.'

Veterinary advisor Simon Adams suggests that part of the reason for Bobby's reluctance to give her up was his concern that the animal rights groups would claim victory. He says: 'One of the problems when trying to broker the release of a circus wild animal is that the charities themselves – to be able to earn money and get the public to say we'll contribute towards this – tend to portray it that they're rescuing the animal from cruelty. This then hardens the circus' attitude. I think this was also a small part of why he didn't want to give her up.' He thinks the main reason is that Bobby wanted to sell Anne and get a better replacement – something Bobby denies. So whether Bobby was digging in his heels to prevent the animal rights groups claiming victory, whether he just wanted some money for her or whether he did genuinely love her remains a mystery.

As to whether or not he was cruel to her – and, maybe more importantly, whether he meant to be cruel to her – it remains as much of a mystery. From the available evidence, we certainly can't conclude that he is a malicious animal beater, given there is nothing but hearsay and conjecture in support of this. He played no role in the horrific beatings which shocked the nation. He did kick Anne's trunk, but it is hardly an act of extreme cruelty. Yes, he employed Nitu, trained him and was ultimately responsible for Anne's welfare as her owner. But there's little to support the idea that he knew what was going on when he wasn't in the barn and had any idea of the depths of Nitu's cruelty towards her. Her living conditions certainly weren't ideal but, as many of those involved in the case argue, they were acceptable when he first started in the circus. Bobby was a man of tradition, a member of a circus dynasty who was respected and revered by the show business world. To accept that everything he had learned and grew up with about animal care was no longer allowed, and that the world had changed around him, would no doubt be a difficult prospect for him. But it may be the version closest to the truth.

CHAPTER 13

BAN WILD ANIMALS IN CIRCUSES

So Anne was finally safe at Longleat and things were looking up. But although life had improved for her, there were many other wild animals still performing in circuses – and, crucially, nothing stopping circuses from bringing in new wild animals, including elephants like Anne. For years, ADI and other animal rights pressure groups and charities had been campaigning to bring in a ban. They hoped Anne – and the public feeling she had whipped up – would prove a catalyst. And they were right. Spurred on by their constituents, MPs battled to get a ban and in 2012, the year after Anne's move, they managed it. The then coalition government vowed to ban all wild animals in circuses by the beginning of 2015. They broke the promise and it has never been implemented, but animal rights groups and MPs maintain the pressure. It was included in the 2015 Tory manifesto.

The public are already firmly in favour. In 2010, 94.5 per cent of the 13,000 who responded to a government consultation on the issue in England called for a ban. And 98 per cent of those who responded in Scotland agreed. The Welsh Assembly also indicated that it would support a ban in Wales. When details of Anne's suffering emerged in 2011, MPs voted to direct ministers to introduce a ban on wild animals in circuses by the following year. The government went to considerable pains to prevent their victory, but the vote ended in a humiliating defeat for them after MPs of all parties unanimously voted for a ban. Campaigners hailed it as an 'historic victory for animal welfare and protection'. Crucially, however, the move was not binding and was not implemented. In 2012, ministers introduced a licensing system as an interim measure – a system branded a costly failure by campaigners. Finally, in 2015, a pledge to outlaw wild animals in circuses appeared in the manifesto of not just the Conservatives, but also Labour, Greens and the DUP in Northern Ireland. But, at the time of writing, nothing has been done about implementing it. Meanwhile, lions, tigers, zebras and camels are still used in travelling circuses despite Prime Minister David Cameron promising to outlaw what he has previously called an 'outdated practice'.

The ban has been supported by a long list of celebrity campaigners including former Beatle Sir Paul McCartney, actors Sir Roger Moore, Judi Dench, Imelda Staunton and Dominic West, musicians Brian May and Moby, model Twiggy and comedians Eddie Izzard, Ricky Gervais and Julian Clary. In a letter to the Prime Minister in July 2015, actor Michael Sheen, whose great-grandmother was a lion tamer, neatly summed up the view of charities and much of the public when he called on the government to implement the ban. On behalf of PETA (People for the Ethical Treatment of Animals), he wrote: 'Wild animals do not voluntarily ride bicycles, stand on their heads or jump through rings of fire. To force animals to perform these meaningless and often uncomfortable or painful tricks, trainers use whips, muzzles, bullhooks and electric prods. The true spirit of the circus is best illustrated by thrilling performances by human entertainers – like clowns and trapeze artists – not by wild animals whose spirits have been broken and who are forced to perform under duress.' Sir Paul McCartney has said previously: 'I hate to see wild animals in circuses. It is heartbreaking to see these poor animals confined in small cages and carted around the country with little respect for their welfare and well-being. I believe an outright ban is long overdue.' Naturalist and television star Bill Oddie also said the practice should be made illegal. Actor Brian Blessed, an ADI supporter, marched on Downing Street to remind David Cameron of the pledge to ban the use of wild circus animals.

Despite having a reputation as being a leader in animal welfare, Britain now lags behind at least twenty-seven countries worldwide who have placed national restrictions on the use of animals in circuses. Countries such as Austria, Belgium, Bolivia, Costa Rica, the Czech Republic, Denmark, Estonia, Finland, Hungary, India, Israel, Luxembourg, Peru, Poland, Portugal, Slovakia, Sweden and Singapore have all limited or banned performing wild animals. Similar discussions are at the time of writing taking place in Brazil, Chile, Colombia, and Greece. Despite there being no nationwide ban yet in Britain, more than 200 local councils have banned the use of wild animals in circuses, though they can still perform on private land. But as a result of the change in the public mood, only three circuses do: Circus Mondao, Peter Jolly's Circus and Thomas Chipperfield's big cat act, though he has not applied for a permit to tour England. Shockingly, while the government has stalled on the issue, there has been an increase in the number of wild animals in circuses.

Animal welfare charities including PETA, the RSPCA, Animal Aid, British Veterinary Association, CAPS, Four Paws, One Kind and World Animal Protection all argue that a ban is desperately needed to prevent European circuses touring round Britain. Gordon Miller from PETA says: 'Unless a ban on the use of animals in circuses is imposed, there's nothing to stop a British circus from acquiring another elephant and putting him or her through a life of torment. The British public have made their support on this issue loud and clear, and there is no longer any excuse for delaying the ban. We hope the new government will respect the will of the people and finally end the suffering of wild animals in circuses. For the sake of animals, the show must not go on.'

When I ask Defra what the current position is, they say: 'We are committed to banning the use of wild animals in circuses and we will do so as soon as parliamentary time allows. Until then, we have a strict licensing system in place to ensure the welfare of any wild animals still being used in circuses in England.' There are currently twenty-four wild animals licensed for use in three travelling circuses in the UK, according to RSPCA figures. The list includes three tigers, two lions, three zebras, a fox, seven reindeer, three snakes – a boa and two Burmese pythons – a racoon, three camels and an Ankole – a breed of African bull with enormous horns. This number has increased from 2013, when there were twenty-one. This, for Dr Ros Clubb, senior scientific officer at the RSPCA, demonstrates the need for a ban. 'I think there's a bit of apathy,' she says. 'It's like, "Oh well, it's dying out anyway, there are only three circuses which have wild animals. It'll just naturally fizzle out". But it hasn't. We've still got big cats in circuses in this country, which is a bit depressing. Their quarters were up in Scotland. It's not very African or Indian weather up there.' She adds that the worst thing is that there is nothing preventing circuses bringing in all the wild animals they want. 'There's nothing to stop anyone coming over and getting a licence under the current system,' she says.

Well-versed in the legal and practical elements of animal welfare, Ros says there is a need for a ban because the current system does not protect wild animals in circuses. She says the Animal Welfare Act in 2006 introduced a duty of care but due to the wording, it only needed to meet what is deemed to be good practice. The problem is, there is no definition of good practice, she says. 'No one has defined what good practice is in the circus. It could be argued that good practice for circuses is meeting the standards set out by the Circus Association. So chaining up an elephant for many hours a day could be seen as good practice in that circumstance. It's a tricky situation. So while an elephant in a zoo that was treated like that could not be seen to meet their needs, it could do in a circus.' She says the RSPCA had struggled with Anne's situation because, legally, they were not convinced they would win proceedings under the terms of the Animal Welfare Act. But when the footage of her being beaten emerged, they had enough.

She is unhappy with the failure to bring in a ban

and unimpressed with the licensing system that has been introduced as an interim measure. Under the current licensing system circuses are subject to at least three inspections a year, including one unannounced inspection, by Defra inspectors under the Welfare of Wild Animals in Travelling Circuses Regulations 2012. The inspectors have to check that welfare licensing conditions are being met and Defra is responsible for enforcing the scheme. The circuses need to appoint a vet with specialist knowledge of the animal, prepare animal records and demonstrate that they can meet the requirements of the licence. The animals need to be inspected by a vet at least once every three months and by a specialist vet at least twice a year. 'I would argue there hasn't been a massive change,' says Ros. 'It's supposed to be an interim measure. The requirements aren't very stringent and if you look at the enclosure sizes that are deemed to be fine in a circus, they're massively smaller than you would see in a zoo, so other than tightening up the paperwork aspect – there might have been tweaks here and there – I don't think there's been a massive change in how they're kept and treated.'

The existing laws don't make much provision for the welfare of animals either. Under the Performing Animals Act 1925, travelling circuses need only register the animals with the local authority. Animals in travelling circuses are also specifically excluded from the Dangerous Wild Animals Act 1976 and the Zoo Licensing Act 1981.

England specifically excluded travelling circuses from an EU regulation covering animal transport, which applies to livestock and zoo animals. This is because England deemed the transporters as the living quarters of the animals. 'It's a weird situation where you've got the same animals being kept but a zoo keeping an elephant behind ticker tape electric fencing would not be approved, while it would be OK in a circus,' says Ros.

ADI believe Anne's suffering led to the pledge to ban wild animals in circuses. Jan Creamer says: 'The good thing about that prosecution is that it did push the MPs to move forward with the ban. About six months later they pushed the government and the government did put a bill together. I know they haven't put the bill before Parliament but they put a bill together.' She says that although there were only about sixteen circuses with animals left in the UK and just three with wild animals, a ban was crucial to prevent European circuses with performing wild animals from coming to the UK.

'A lot of people say why bother if there are so few,' says Jan. 'But they'll all come over from Europe. The reason the European circuses aren't bringing over all their wild animals is because they know they're not welcome here. We've got about 200 local bans in the UK – they ban either all animals or wild animals from council-owned land – and that was done in the seventies and eighties. We can remember just a few years ago an Italian circus brought a rhino here and it was only the protests that discouraged it and it went over to Ireland and then straight back to Italy. But those European animals will be brought here if we don't ban because it's an opportunity for them.'

Tim Phillips adds: 'You cannot place animal welfare in the hands of it constantly being in the newspapers. Circuses with animals will come back. Most people wouldn't dream of going to a dog fight but there's a reason we ban it – because there are a few headcases who will. When these truly majestic animals – whether it's horses or whether it's elephants, lions and tigers – are kept in the most substandard conditions, and we know now that violence in trailers is endemic, what hope do we have for any other animals if we just say: "Oh, there's only a few of them doing it, let them do it."'

At the time of writing, the ban still hasn't been implemented, but animal rights groups keep up the fight to ensure a situation like Anne's never occurs again.

CHAPTER 14

HAPPY ENDING

Having made it to the ripe old age of sixty, Anne was due an upgrade on her living quarters at Longleat and Anne's Haven was finally built in 2015. The elephant house is more than most of us could dream of: a £1.2 million mansion with nearly two acres of private garden and its own plunge pool. And when she gets bored of her own enclosure, she can always gaze out on the Grade I-listed undulating parkland designed by Capability Brown. She is overlooked only by flamingos and a few deer, and while there are lots of humans who wander past, she can always retreat inside her barn, where the public can't see her.

Perhaps a fitting introduction to how much her health

has improved since she moved to Longleat was her journey to her new home in February 2015. Her keepers were planning to transport her 800 metres from the old to the new house in a vehicle, but on the morning of the transfer they decided to allow her the chance to make the journey herself, it being good weather. They thought that it would take her around five hours with a pause halfway, but, incredibly, she did it within an hour with no stop. Everyone was amazed. 'We'd expected it would take several hours,' says Jon Cracknell of Longleat, 'with a stop halfway to let her rest and have a drink, but it was as if she was excited to get to her new place – she did it in one go.' Once there, she needed a good rest. 'For her, it was a marathon,' he adds. But soon she was ready to explore.

Inside the house, there are nearly 1,000 square metres of deep sand floors as well as heating, which keeps her at a comfortable 18 degrees. She shares her home, which members of the public donated £410,000 to build, with three inquisitive Anglo-Nubian goats named Costa, Coffee and Sugar, and three full-time keepers – Kevin Nibbs, Ross Ellis and Luke Walker – who attend to her every whim. Inside, there are deep sand floors that should be easier on her legs, more than twenty natural skylight panels so it isn't dark when she chooses to stay inside, automated feeding systems and drinking canisters, which refill themselves. There is also an area for medical treatment. For her amusement, there are rocks, log piles and a sandpit in the enclosure, as well as a number of toys. Her favourites include a boomer ball (a large plastic ball on a rope), a scratching post for her skin, and a game known as KerTrunk – based on the family game KerPlunk – in which she can retrieve food from a large tube by removing the correct pole. Her keepers are most proud of having devised this game, which she quickly got the hang of, and the concept has now spread round Longleat, they tell me. Her keeper Ross Ellis says she is a huge show-off and very clever – sometimes even challenging her keepers. 'She loves an audience,' he says. 'She's very intelligent, too. We're constantly thinking up new toys to keep her stimulated and active. But it's a war of minds. We come up with a new game such as KerTrunk that we think will take her a couple of days to figure out, and within a few minutes she's worked it out.' They also say that she loves Heart and Classic FM on the radio.

Anne's day-to-day regime sounds something like living at an elephant version of Claridge's. She awakes to an 8kg breakfast at 8.30am, consisting of corn and fibre with vitamin and mineral supplements to help with her arthritis, though she has to be quick as the goats often attempt to steal it. Hay is also placed in cargo nets in the ceiling and then dropped down at random times throughout the day so she can snack. After breakfast, she has a warm water 'power shower' with a pressure washer and then she's left to play, relax and destroy things – which seems to be her favourite pastime. Tea-time is at 3.30pm and she's served a bale of hay, which she likes to dip in her water as if it were a biscuit in a mug of tea. After her keepers go home at the end of her day, she is left alone with a nightlight so it's not entirely dark. She will sleep for around five hours at a time, according to her keepers, who watch her on CCTV from one of the many cameras in the barn. Sometimes, she even goes out for a night-time stroll when no one is there to see her. Her favourite pastimes include rolling in the mud and digging. Her keeper Ross says she eats most things except for parsnips. 'Her favourite foods are carrots, bananas and oranges,' he says, 'but she will not even entertain a parsnip. She cannot stand parsnips.'

It is hoped that the three goats will provide some stimulation for Anne. Her keepers believe they are confident and inquisitive enough to provide interaction and companionship for her, but small enough not to risk bullying or harming her. 'At first we wondered about introducing sheep, but if Anne got cross, she could grab their fleece with her trunk, while dogs might bite her or become aggressive,' Jon Cracknell told the *Daily Mail*. 'Goats, on the other hand, are inquisitive creatures, so they would provide a level of suitable interaction. They don't have horns so they can't do her any damage. They're already providing some interaction, although they will steal her food if she's not quick enough. We make sure they're out of the way when she is having her meals.' He adds: 'When you watch them, you won't see them interact much but if you watch them on TV when they sleep together, they work well together.' Showing me a video of a day in Anne's life, on fast forward – 'there are cameras everywhere,' he adds, with a knowing look – he points out her interaction with them. 'What the goats do is nick her food off the floor so now she's changed her behaviour and interacts more. She'll actually get food and put it on the ground and step on it, so they can't get it. So they do stimulate her a bit.'

Not only is her comfort assured, her health is also well attended to. As well as her three full-time keepers, Anne is regularly visited by vets. She still has her three-weekly osteopath appointments with Tony Nevin too. I ask him about the difficulties of giving her treatments under the protected contact system, which means they can't force her to do anything she doesn't want to. But apparently it's a very easy process. 'She's food-orientated so you lure her with treats,' he explains. 'Lots of fresh fruit and veg and she's anyone's friend. She's ruled by her stomach, that one.' He also says she is always happy to be treated by him. 'She seems to enjoy the treatment. Palpably. She always comes up and is waiting when she sees me. From that point of view, it's quite flattering,' he says. The new system suits her, he says, and adds: 'She's like your grandparent. They don't always want to go out, they don't want to do much. They don't want to see visitors sometimes. I don't think she gets that lonely, to be honest. I think she's quite happy on her own.'

Asked about Anne's future prospects, Tony pauses for a moment. 'She's in her twilight years,' he resumes, 'and with each month that goes by you're always wondering but there's nothing to suggest anything other than she's an old elephant. We'll just keep plodding along, doing the same as we have been: maintaining her weight, me with her body framework, the vet monitoring her health and the keepers monitoring everything else.'

Her new home has also been specially designed to meet a lot of her health needs. When she first arrived at Longleat, Anne was unable to lift up her trunk as she'd always had her food served to her on the ground, so had lost the full use of it. So Longleat gradually started putting her food in higher places and hanging holders from the ceiling so she could start using the muscle more. Her trunk has drastically improved as a result. 'Before, what she used to do was flip her trunk up on the metal work and walk along and then get to the hay and knock it down,' Jon explains. 'Now, she physically has to go right up and grab from the feeders and she can do that. And even just moving to the new house with the new feeders has helped her to improve and that trunk, I would say, is not far from being back to what it should be in a normal elephant.' From what tests Longleat can do – scanning elephants is always a tad difficult, given their size – she seems to be in good health, but her back legs are an ongoing problem. She'll have to be supported with pain relief for the rest of her life and she will never be able to lift her hind leg and will always drag it, but at last, she can lie down. She lies on the big sand piles in her enclosure and rubs against them. 'That's one of the big things,' says Jon. 'There are elephants in zoos in Europe that haven't laid down for ten years. They are supposed to; they should have the option.'

But instead of adoring gratitude for her luxurious new life, Anne, as always, hilariously, has other plans. Jon told the *Daily Mail* at the time: 'When we moved her into the new enclosure, the first thing she did was to go around the pen checking all the nuts, bolts and padlocks. She even unscrewed a few – just to show us she could. Elephants are incredibly dexterous with their trunks: they can pick up a grain of rice if they want – it's like their little finger.' She has also lost none of her mischief. Her keepers tell me she has a tricky habit of tying visitors' shoelaces together when they aren't watching. Once, she also fleetingly attempted to climb a wall in her new enclosure, leaving huge marks up the wall, to the despair of her keepers. And she regularly destroys the carefully constructed games that they spend hours devising.

'We had a big tyre that we needed to put in and it took an hour or so just to move it an inch,' says Ross. 'It took a week to get it in place but she came in and moved it in two seconds.'

Ryan Hockley, head of safari and her former keeper, recalls similar issues: 'Every Halloween we make carved pumpkins for her. But she's like: "I hate your stupid pumpkins" and goes around smashing them up. Maybe it's because she was never allowed to smash the circus up.' Ross adds: 'There was this log we had and she kept attacking it for a couple of days. Then finally it cracked. She looked at it and you could see from her face she was thinking: "Oh God, what have I done?" But we just laughed about it. She is subtly full of beans, a mischievous little mare. But we think she's a duchess. When she thinks there's no one looking, she's actually very gentle.

'Over the past week when it's been really hot we made some ice blocks for her. We were well chuffed with them and we put fruit and veg in. I put one up the other day and it took about ten minutes to get it up because it was awkward and I said: "Anne, check this out," and that was it. I had no time to take a photo; it was gone. She gave me a little rumble and wandered off. So what takes an hour to make takes a minute to destroy.' I ask him about the noise she makes. He says: 'It's really bassy, it's sweet. She trumpets for us sometimes.'

One of the key features of Anne's new home is that it is designed so she has no direct interaction with humans. This is now the design standard for elephants in captivity across the Western world. It means, crucially, no need for bullhooks or chains; it also means that the animals can make their own decisions about what they participate in. There is a four-metre perimeter 'safe' area for staff and a treatment area where her toenails can be clipped and her health can be assessed.

Her keepers weren't initially thrilled with this prospect. Ross says: 'She's always been free contact. I worried she was going to think she's done something wrong when we became protected contact. She loved interaction when she was free contact.' But they've gradually decided that it's actually better. Anne is taught using sticks with 'targets' – painted tennis balls – on the end. She is bribed with food to learn to associate words with actions. Ross says: 'We put a target on the floor and she's got to lift her foot so we can check her footwork. The whole thing takes ages to teach her. When she does it right, you go ecstatic, mental, boasting about how well she's done. She likes that. I do that when she's had a really good session. She's just really, really clever.'

The design of the new house gives Anne the freedom to choose whether or not to interact with humans and whether or not she wants to be inside or outside. 'It wasn't ideal in that [the old] house,' Jon explains. 'She couldn't go in and out like she can now because the house was what it was: it was an emergency thing. It was supposed to be shorter term than it was, and that is something we failed on but that's rectified now.' He adds that she picked up on the concept of protected contact really quickly – 'almost quicker than the staff, actually,' he jokes. He also says that she is so easily trained that she could probably still do a tub stand, though he quickly dismisses the idea, adding: 'It's not something we would ever look at, but she's smart, she knows it all. She remembers it.'

But there are plenty of people who have taken Anne's story to their hearts and have very strong opinions about how she should best be cared for. Jon says he spends a lot of his time responding to people on the safari park's Facebook page and answering questions, complaints and sometimes accusations. 'I spend something like 10 per cent of my time just on Anne, it's insane,' he says. The team are regularly contacted by people concerned about Anne's welfare and her lack of companionship. They say they respond as best they can and invite the complainants to Longleat, if necessary, to see her in her new home.

But the real test of whether or not they have succeeded is the official one. BIAZA (British and Irish Association of Zoos and Aquariums) has scored Longleat 95 per cent on their elephant audit. Dr Kirsten Pullen, BIAZA's CEO, said: 'Despite the challenges presented by Anne's background, we are delighted that Longleat Safari Park have achieved an excellent result of 95 per cent compliance in the 2015 BIAZA Elephant Facilities and Management Audit.' She said that the staff and management had shown 'a dedicated and conscientious approach to achieving the best for Anne's health and welfare.' Jon says that BIAZA score on how well certain criteria are met. Longleat lost 5 per cent because Anne is on her own, he adds.

Sadly, because of Anne's age and health, euthanasia has to be an option, should she ever be found to be in too much pain. 'We've considered euthanasia, we've got a euthanasia plan and we've got criteria for it,' says Jon, 'but she doesn't meet them. We've had moments where we've thought: "Is it time?" and it isn't, so we do have a very strict policy of what to do. We're hoping, as anyone would, that she's just going to lie down and not wake up one day and that's an easier way out, but it's our responsibility to Anne that we have these policies in place, because if it comes to a point where she is down or she can't get up or her leg goes, then we're ready. So there's a cupboard – we've got drugs, we're ready to go. If her leg literally snaps, because we don't know what's going on in there and we couldn't do anything for it, we're not going to sit round with crystals and singing hymns until she dies naturally a week later.'

Hopefully, though, it won't come to this.

When I last checked in on Anne in July 2015, she had access to her full paddock, which is now completely finished, and had gone for a wander to its farthest reaches. She has access to a pool in which she takes occasional dips. The enclosure is overlooked by monkeys, camels, Ankole cattle and rhinos – but, thankfully, no pelicans.

Her home is also historic, having been built on an area once used as an American military field hospital during the Second World War. She has uninterrupted views of the eighteenth-century parkland, rolling hills, specimen trees and woodland. Longleat tell me that she has been enjoying the summer and indulging in mud baths.

Her keeper Ross says he can't believe the transformation in her. 'I'd never worked with elephants but even I could see straight away that she was very, very nervy about everything,' he says. 'If you were near her, no matter what you were doing, she'd keep her eyes on you but if you looked at her, she'd look away. It was that blatant and you could see that. And that's why now it's the best place in the world because now she looks us in the eye. She's interested in what we're doing. You can see the change in her is massive, it's lovely to see.'

In the meantime, Anne is happy to play and relax all day and to take things easy after fifty years of hard graft. When I last saw her, she was a picture of contentment, happily pottering around her shed. I fed her bananas, which she seemed delighted with, grabbing them with her dexterous trunk and then shovelling them into her mouth, and her eyes seemed to twinkle as she watched me. Her keepers seemed friendly and happy and she in turn seemed relaxed with them and although she mostly ignores the goats, she is clearly content in their company. Most days she chooses to stay indoors, her keepers say, out of the public eye and with no need to even think about performing. Instead she prefers to pick at her hay and relax. As the sun sets on a warm and balmy day at Longleat and I leave for home, I look back towards her enclosure. There is no sign of her. She's inside, away from the audience. The curtains have finally come down on her after more than fifty years of performance and she can finally retire from the spotlight. I can't help but smile to myself.

Finally, she is free.